Racing to a Cryptocurrency Future:

Facebook, China & the Future of a Trustless World

Juncheng Zhang

Racing to a Cryptocurrency Future:
Facebook, China & the Future of a Trustless World
Copyright @ 2010
Published Independently

1st Edition, 1st Revision (April 2020)

ISBN-13: 979-8-640-81408-8

CONTENTS

BACKGROUND

Blockchain is the underlying technology of Bitcoin, the cryptocurrency invented in 2008 by the pseudonymous "Satoshi Nakamoto". On the Halloween of 2008, the figure under the Japanese pseudonym announced Bitcoin through an email entitled "Bitcoin P2P e-cash paper" to a tight cryptography enthusiast circle called "The Cryptography Mailing List." Over the past decade, despite the heavy skepticism from the public and legal issues with governments across the world, Bitcoin has grown from a small open-sourced project into an international phenomenon worth of billions of dollars, and its underlying technology, blockchain, has given rise to many revolutionary concepts to solve long-standing social issues and create valuable opportunities for social progress. From universal basic income to Internet privacy, from international monetary transaction to global currency, many people's lives were pulled closer to each other as a result of

Bitcoin and blockchain, with new promises to take the power of Internet to the next level. These new promises opened windows for innovation, which drove new waves of capital investment into what investors believed to be the next-generation billion-dollar projects. Under the flashy titles of "decentralized," "permissionless," "trustless," and "low transaction fee," many projects took off with huge rounds of funding that aimed to be the Amazon of the "blockchain age". "Decentralize everything" has become the banner of a great many of blockchain enthusiasts who see flaws in the existing Internet infrastructure.

With a fervor only rivaled by that during the dotcom bubble, the blockchain valuation market went through several rise-and-crash cycles, indicative of what have been the public opinion of the technology over the same period: total public ignorance, mockery, regulatory pressure, market bearish pessimism, and finally world-wide recognition. In late 2017, during the peaking of the cryptocurrency market, it might have been called a bubble, a fraud, or "rat poison squared,"[1] but in 2019, with recognition from many governments and a more matured technology, particularly from China's President Xi Jinping during a Politburo Meeting in October 2019, who considered blockchain as "an important window for breakthrough in the independent innovation of key technologies,"[2] both industry veterans and curious newcomers admit that it is here to stay. The story is, even in failed states such as Venezuela and war-torn countries like Syria, even though they do not have shelter or food, where they have a cellphone connected online, they have Bitcoin; and even when you do not have Bitcoin, you know you should know how blockchain works.

It is important to clarify important questions and expel the myth around this technology, now that we are in the 11th year of the technology, before we move forward to analyzing and commenting on the current progress made in the area. First, in many areas, the promises and the excitement around the technology are entirely not unfounded - it has to do with the problem that it solved. The reason why the blockchain technology is revolutionary is that it successfully solves what in digital currency is known as the "double-spending" problem: the problem that the same piece of digital asset is spent twice by the holder or spent in the form of a duplicate while the original copy is retained. To be more precise, blockchain solved the problem without relying on a third party which is trusted to make sure that the asset is spent and managed correctly and that the spending records are not tempered with. By eliminating a third party in the process and transferring the trust from a human-managed entity to the cryptographic technology, security risks are reduced and trust in the process is more transparent to users.

Although this issue does not exist in paper currency as each dollar bill is unique in its existence by definition, fiat currency in its digital form still needs a way to prevent such problems. The traditional solution to double-spending is through a centralized third party, usually a bank, which maintains what is known as a digital "ledger" - essentially a book for recording transactions between accounts. The bank makes money because it has the trust of the customer to safe keep the ledger and are willing to put their money on the ledger of this particular entity. This is known as the centralized solution, and for thousands of years in its existence, it has not only been the way banking is conducted but has been copied in almost every other industry, from the email platforms that manage the transferring of our messages, to social media platforms that store our online social life, and to government agencies where citizens' identity are kept. These are all very sensitive information that companies spend billions of dollars in database security to protect but sometimes fail. Anyone with access to the information ultimately has the ability to "hack" into someone's life and cause serious damage in sophisticated ways, while the victim remains unaware until after the matter. Any company with such a large collection of personal data could easily turn this "knowledge" into profit, by selling the data that users are willing to give in exchange for the services the company provides to the people and businesses that deem the information valuable. As a result, for thousands of years, the people controlling these centralized entities have been

4

the ones in society with most power. When such power gets too concentrated, sections of populations would start to resist and address this inequality in power distribution. When such effort succeeds, it is called a revolution.

It is, therefore, no surprise that the blockchain technology has been branded among other disrupted and revolutionary technologies, because for the first time in a long time, it offered a decentralized solution to the trust issue: not one but multiple entities can participate in securing and updating the database where sensitive information is stored such that a distributed trust is created. In fact, although it might be the first time that decentralization of power and authority has happened in technology, it is certainly not the first time it has happened in history. Historically government, or the state, in charge of making organizational policies with its philosophy and values guiding the policy-making written in the form of its constitution, has been the most powerful institution in society (although there was a time when the Church yielded control over the government as well). But there was a period in time when power was concentrated in one monarch passed down from their family member. It was not until the ancient Greek and Romans that the power was distributed to a larger number of people, most of whom were elected by the public. Some monarchies lasted longer than others, and there are still some left today, but from the larger picture, the historic trend seems to be that power tends to decentralize. If we divide our life into the physical world, the world which our current physiological senses can perceive and interact with, and the virtual world, the world with which we need to interact through the medium of artificial instruments such as a computer and the Internet, what blockchain does is to decentralize the virtual one. In such stage of development of human civilization, where more and more of our life is conducted through the virtual world, that is significant.

However, although the movement to decentralize power has much popular support, there are many areas in society that still have the elements and features of more or less centralized power. It is actually an interesting phenomenon in the contemporary world that while public authorities such as the government in many countries are elected democratically, the power of smaller institutions in different areas of society is usually concentrated in the rooms of board members. Democratic processes that make the government processes transparent to a certain degree are lacked in business. When public interest is not represented in the power distribution, the public starts to intervene. The result is the need for governmental supervision and regulation to balance the scale of power between the public and the corporation.

Nevertheless, sometimes the one corporation gets powerful enough so that it has the resources and technological capabilities to develop technologies fast enough that the government would fail to catch up with its social and political implications and issue relevant regulatory laws until public interest has been compromised. Furthermore, such corporate entities provide services so comprehensive now that every aspect of our life gets stored in some digital form through their platforms. While some see the benefits of such progress, some voice their concerns on the scale of such companies. As recently illustrated by Facebook's Cambridge Analytica scandal, the lack of transparency and public oversight in what can only be called monopolies in certain public domains has called for new government regulations to be put in place to balance the growing control of tech companies in public life.

This is a unique phenomenon in the information age, as technological innovations make more and more public domains no longer subject to the sole governance of public institutions, but open to free market competition of tech startups. Technology companies now govern these newly created virtual public domains, opening up a second front where political battles are fought and public attention is spent. What used to be a public-government power dichotomy has now become public vs. tech corporation dichotomy, a new frontier where public interest is discussed and defended. This intrusion by the free-market driven tech corporations into what used to be solely government-occupied areas has caused political division in both the U.S. and Europe as to whether the power of tech companies should be restricted by government intervention. That is, many argue that a "bigger government" is needed to counter-balance the forces of tech. From European Union's General Data Privacy Regulation [3] implemented in 2018 to ensure user consent to the data collection by online platforms, to the numerous congressional and senatorial hearings on Facebook's plan to establish a global currency and payment system, new technologies keep pushing the boundary between government and tech innovation.

It is to be noted that, when technology is used for solving practical social problems, a positive stance by a government toward technology adoption in society has a lot of beneficial social implications such as reducing poverty and improving living standard. The wide adoption of digital wallets such as PayPal has greatly expedited the speed at which businesses conduct transactions, the creation of YouTube has enabled a greater representation of public opinion in politics without having to go through laborious processes of government bureaucracy, and the creation of e-commerce platforms have created hundreds of thousands of jobs for individual business owners. If one considers that the world has a limitless number of problems to solve, then technology could potentially provide an unlimited number of solutions. It is therefore no coincidence that Bitcoin was announced shortly after the catastrophic failure of the capitalist system in the West as a decentralized solution to the modern financial system. One could also easily argue for other blockchain-based solutions to address the problems that the current sovereign financial system has failed at, such as providing financial infrastructure for millions in the unbanked Africa – the initiative led by the aforementioned Facebook's Libra.

Such is one implication of the advancement of technological innovations to modern social problems. That is, while the public and the regulators pay attention to the pitfalls of innovative technologies, policymakers should also avoid the mistake of protecting public interest at the expense of stifling innovation, which would ultimately be more harmful to damage the public interest. In the end, innovation, wasted, results in lost opportunities and lack of means to economic progress. The rise of cryptocurrency presents challenges like this to regulators and policymakers.

While discussing the future that innovative technologies present to human society, one must not ignore the national interest at play that is both independent and related to the domestic interest in a given society. Viewing technological progress from an international point of view would hence require us to see development of technology as means to enhance national power in the international stage, putting the consequence of succeeding or failing to develop a technology due to domestic interest in the context of international power dynamics. History has taught us that an advantage in a key technology could bolster a nation's power to a position of global dominance, as best exemplified by the nuclear dominance of the U.S. in the 40s and 50s. For other countries in a less prominent position, having an edge in new technologies could unleash a new wave of economic growth and freedom from dependence on foreign economies. Put in perspective, blockchain is not only a subject of discussion between the public and the government, but also a strategic point for contention between governments. It is up to the individual government in different countries to decide what kind of stance they take toward this kind of tech innovation, taking into account both the domestic politics and international interests.

In the blockchain industry, if we view the current relationship between innovators and regulators in the U.S. as one of a restrictive nature, then a study on a country-to-country basis would reveal a more dynamic picture. While the U.S. government views blockchain largely as a tool for tech giants to challenge the sovereign power of the U.S. government and an excuse to further violate public interest, countries such as China view the technology as an opportunity to establish a more efficient domestic economy and a new platform for global finance[4]. Not only does China warrant state support for blockchain, but the goal of such initiative is aimed at solving both domestic problems and establishing international credibility. What kind of geopolitical implications would such an initiative taken by China have on the international financial system? How would a Chinese fiat-based cryptocurrency alter the global trading dynamics? These are just some of the many questions that have recently emerged and remained unanswered and largely undiscussed.

The stark contrast between the response to blockchain innovation in the domestic U.S. and state-led China reveals the many problems of social media's role in domestic U.S. The problematic and dramatic relationship between companies such as Facebook and Twitter and political leaders leaves us much to think about in terms of the corporate governance structure that controls these platforms. Without solving this issue, distrust between big tech companies and the government would be a continuing problem that obstructs the progress in tech innovation. One potential solution to reconcile the conflict between public movement and corporate management is to establish public trust in the corporate governance structure. That is, to decentralize corporate governance structure and establish measures of public forum and intervention. Speaking in political terms, there lacks a way for the public in the decision-making processes within the management of the tech platforms. The magnitude of this need is reflected by the scale at which public discourse is disseminated and moderated online. The extent to which these platforms constitute a public good given the amount of influence the

11

decisions made by the corporate management level have on the direction public discourse progresses makes for a case as to exactly how much public intervention is needed in the modern corporate world. Clearly, although there are still voices in support of a total free-market solution to these information-age debates, clearly the public pushback has reached a level unprecedented before. Exactly how much direct public opinion over the decision-making process in tech companies should be warranted in a way that does not impede innovation at the danger of public opinion deadlock becomes a relevant question more than ever.

In essence, the possession of power comes under scrutiny. In an industry where products are produced independent of public discourse, it is less of a problem, but in an industry where public discourse is a direct product of the company, more interests are at stake. A direct manifestation of these interests in political discourse is democratic representation of different interest groups that decentralize the state power into multiple factions. The means to achieve this has historically been the parliament or the congress/senate of a government, where public interest is represented at the vote of their representatives. The current situation on political discourse has called for a similar effort made in the corporate world. Certainly, any framework proposed to decentralize corporate power would be necessarily complicated due to the complex financial forces at play in the corporate world. Exactly how financial interests should be represented in an efficient and effective distributed model that could provide an alternative to the centralized shareholder model that the current corporate world offers. For a long time, the decentralizing power of the Internet was thought to be the answer: PayPal was created to move money online, Napster made music digital, YouTube made video sharing a status quo, Yahoo brought emailing to the masses, Google further democratized and demonetized information, but they were still built on the previous shareholder model. It was not until the invention of blockchain that new solutions have been proposed. Decentralized governance models based on *"tokens"* – a unit of participation in the governance - have given rise to models such as Delegated Proof-of-Stake (DPOS), a *"consensus mechanism"* through which the current state of the network is determined by tokens or other forms of measure of power. Thus, a whole subject of *"Tokenomics"* [5] has therefore been born to study these decentralized governance models.

It is to be noted that Bitcoin's consensus model, Proof-of-Work (POW), was the first mechanism created, but, so far, many more consensus mechanisms have joined the ranks of PO, acting as an integral part of different blockchain networks. From Proof-of-Work to Delegated Proof-of-Stake (DPOS) in EOS, these new models propose that "power" could be earned not just by financial resources, but by the amount of work contributed to a system. Such model directly proposes a huge challenge to the current form of government where the wealthy controls the majority of society's resources and inequality is extremely high. Blockchain presents us with such an opportunity to balance the scale.

Ultimately, the question is whether technology could enhance social justice, reduce inequality, and establish more public trust. The great problem of democracy – how to increase voter participation in elections and transparency in governance processes – offers us a sobering look into the areas for improvement. The current political atmosphere in many democracies are plagued with decreasing voter turnout and lack of accountability and transparency in government processes. Many of the government programs suffer from low efficiency experience many logistic issues during implementation. On other areas such as healthcare and citizen identity management, the notorious crash of Obama's healthcare website showed the negligence and the inexperience of the government in managing national infrastructure digitally on a large scale. From voting to ID, from residency to healthcare, the evidence points to a huge deficiency in digitalization in government infrastructure and for a credibility-through-transparency technology to establish public trust. While on the civilian level, technology has enabled great efficiency, it remains to be seen as to how technology can counter the bureaucracy and logistical difficulties in politics. In many ways, political institutions these days are still using the 20th century solutions to 21st century problems.

Blockchain presents many solutions to these problems. The inherent transparency and security that it offers makes it an ideal candidate to set up systems that the public can interact with efficiently, saving time and extra maintenance expenses. In the U.S., for example, where partisan feuds have led to public misinformation, mistrust and confusion on the integrity of key data on democratic processes, blockchain technology could present interesting solutions worth considering.

In fact, transparency and security through use of blockchain has been proven in several future-faring countries and has earned critical praise, with Estonia and China both offering us a unique window into how blockchain could enhance government performance and public trust in small and large countries respectively. However, the popularization of the technology still faces many challenges in reality. These problems are as much technological as much political. Why would a political system that feeds on bipartisan opposition, for example, adopt such a system, is one of the questions worth asking. Another one is on who would be the leader – the strongman leader, so to speak – to take such initiative? Ultimately, what kind of political atmosphere would welcome the introduction of such tools. These are the human questions we need to ask in the age of technology.

Hence what exactly does the kind of future look like? One that has made millions of blockchain and cryptocurrency enthusiasts and government policymakers around the world excited about the technology. We know that the market boom in cryptocurrency over the past few years in cryptocurrency fueled a lot of that excitement that resulted from short-term speculative mania, but how exactly is blockchain making society a more efficient, happier place by measurable standards? The wealth it could create, for example, and the distribution of wealth it could be used for. That is, how blockchain would help us create this abundance and the distribution of abundance in and on the road to a post-abundance society – these are important questions political thinkers, economists and, more recently, technologists have endeavored to answer, and we know that some of their answers have provided key insights into how innovations with the power to decentralize and redistribute abundance, the exact likes of which like blockchain, would transform our world.

By analyzing the two most important aspects of blockchain's innovation – decentralized trust and its financial application – we can connect the dots with efforts that were made in recent history to decentralize power and to redistribute wealth, thus shining light on the future that blockchain brings to us. In many areas, decentralized governance proposes a framework of governance similar to what we have in blockchain as DAO (Decentralized Autonomous Organization) or DAC (Decentralized Autonomous Corporation): an organization/corporation whose rules are encoded and whose governance is controlled by its shareholders, not a central government. In both cases, centralized brainpower gives way to individual autonomy, and the raison d'étre and also the practical necessity of a central governing body is seriously challenged. In a sense, blockchain is creating a democracy for the internet.

It is, therefore, interesting that the individual autonomy as the basic governance unit to form an organized, productive group without the need for a central guiding body emerged as a political movement in the first half of the 20th century and is implemented again through technological means approximately a century later. This form of organization - politically known as libertarian democracy - has provided a genuinely refreshing alternative solution to the problems that exist in the predominant form of social organizations that we have today, namely centralized decision-making bodies. For example, many of today's multinational corporations have incited much public outcry with regard to their political influence, environmental policy, and financial structure. The American public has been calling for closing in the gap between how much a CEO of a large company gets compensated and how little the company's lower level staff get paid. The truth is that although the organization is still productive and functional, the consequence is a form of inequality that causes many social problems. Without internal representation, it is hard to see how meaningful changes could be made without some form of enforceable external intervention, as capitalistic tendencies generally lead to concentration of wealth in a minority of the population. As a result, how DAO could provide an alternative governing system that distributes wealth and power in a way that is socially accountable, responsive, and productive becomes a relevant subject for discussion today. We shall explore this subject in the fifth chapter.

Another area that is worth discussing with respect to the governance in the digital age is the use of big data and artificial intelligence in governance decision-making processes, to enhance the quality of the policies being made and improve the results of the implementation.
A traffic system with an AI analytics system in a city, for example, could diagnose the parts of road that are congested and automatically generate an alternative route for the traffic with the data that the system is constantly collecting from all parts of the road network, therefore alleviating the congestion issue. A policy-making process without the aid of big data, is like the traffic system without the AI analytics – you may reach the destination eventually, but with much higher cost of time and other resources.

Similarly, if policies were to have the highest level of efficiency and effectiveness on society, they must be guided by data collected from all sections of the economy and social groups. This is the same logic behind the user data collection for which technology companies are notorious for, but the accuracy of which is largely praised, as it significantly reduces the risks that businesses and government bodies take in implementing their strategies.

Integrating artificial intelligence into a decentralized blockchain governance system, therefore, would give the governance body a sense of direction which is reliably support by data from the activities in the blockchain network, be it transaction data, network load, or user number, which then dictate whether the network capacity needs to be increased, where in the network optimization is needed, and what the projected growth of the network is. All this becomes especially pertinent when the blockchain is a one where currency is issued, and major macroeconomic adjustments affect the lives of a large number of people. In a future where a global transaction system exists on blockchain, or multiple financial systems communicate through different blockchain networks, an integration with artificial intelligence could significantly reduce the risk of high inflation and unwanted acts of currency manipulation. This topic attaches right onto the edge of what is called the "Fourth Industrial Revolution," which covers "wide-ranging fields such as artificial intelligence (AI), robotics, the Internet of things (IoT), autonomous vehicles, 3D printing, nanotechnology, biotechnology, materials science, energy storage and quantum computing, to name a few."[7]

Blockchain, among these technologies, gained momentum relatively recently, which means that it has a nascent market that is more prone to speculation and a technological prospect that gives a more long-term outlook. Exactly how it fits into the larger picture of the new industrial revolution is the question that determines the fate of the technology, an enigma into which huge sums of R&D budget is being poured into by corporations and governments to decrypt. The magnitude of the occurrence of a single industrial revolution lies in the fundamental change in the productive forces and the production relations that innovation causes in society. From robots that replace human assembly line, to AI that conducts market analytics, to blockchain that replaces centralized trust, the world is undergoing a tectonic shift in socially and economically, and blockchain is but one component of this shift. Whoever manages to gain a lead in the development of such technologies will reap the benefits to their advantage. Government or individual, they understand that history has generously rewarded the pioneers, launching them into prosperity, and given little to the late comers, leaving them in a struggle for survival. It is indeed a race that we are in. How will the world change because of this?

In this book, we attempt to answer this question by looking at three of the most prominent events that have taken place because of the invention of blockchain and cryptocurrency: Facebook's Libra, China's central bank's cryptocurrency, and the blockchain project with the largest public fundraise in the industry's history. We examine the political as well as the economic implications of these events locally and internationally. These innovative actors from both the public and the private sector will give us a short but deep peak into the future that is unfolding. Welcome to *Racing to a Cryptocurrency Future: Facebook, China, and the Future of a Trustless World.*

The following section of the book is a brief analysis on some of the arguments from blockchain critics that have been proven wrong by the progress in blockchain and, and explanations why their wrongful indictments inevitably failed to reflect the reality of the technologies, as we see often in the static thinking many are trapped in facing new changes.

Failure to embrace new technologies could lead to career obstacles for individual, bankruptcy for corporations, dominance by others for nations, and lack of prosperity for human society.

"People don't like change, but you need to embrace change if the alternative is disaster."
— Elon Musk

PRELUDE

Why & Where the Critics Are Wrong

Before we delve into the subject, I believe it is important to clear out some of the misunderstandings that public has had over cryptocurrency and blockchain. Blockchain is no different from other previous emerging technologies, in the sense that the confusion and misunderstanding surrounding it in the initial phases of its emergence blocked the public imagination of the true potential of the technology. If we are going to have an honest discussion of the impact of this technology of our future, anyone starting the discussion should take it upon themselves to address the criticisms and lay a mutual common ground first. Therefore, before we proceed further, let's take some time to answer some of the doubts you might have on our subject matter here that is blockchain and cryptocurrency. I do not suggest you skip this section unless you are an industry veteran.

Concrete criticisms have been launched against cryptocurrency and blockchain in the short history of the technology. To marshal fair analytical responses to these criticisms, we must first concede that the critics do have solid evidence on the many areas that they had pointed out to be problematic. It is, in fact, that they would still eventually be proven wrong about the blockchain industry despite the validity of some of their criticisms, not because of lack of validity in their claims. However, these criticisms would not amount to the total demise of the blockchain technology – at least so far such tendencies yet to be seen on a large scale – but to cause the industry to become more aware of the "danger zones" that could damage their progress and public perception and to innovate to respond to such criticisms.

One of the more direct criticisms against blockchain technology is best illustrated by a 2017 article entitled "Ten Years in, nobody has come up a use for blockchain,"[1] which pointed out the lack of practical, effective applications of blockchain that solve problems, a sharp contrast to the early promises made by industry pioneers to "change everything." Although one could characterize it as an "overpromise-under-deliver" scenario, typical in many tech startups these days, it is not entirely the fault of one side. To understand the extent of the disappointment the market had on the existing applications of blockchain, one should not forget what kind of unrealistic market expectations set up by already mature Internet industry.

The Internet Boom in the 90s and early 2000s resulted in a large number of IPOs among the Internet startups, some of which became the very technology companies that make up the majority of today's technology scene. Their applications have grown from small platforms with poor user experience, to global platforms with a range of services that extend to every corner of the civic life. The Internet revolution has absolutely revolutionized our life. However, with a few companies practically dominating the scene, an illusion has been created that any revolutionary technology has to achieve the scale of those companies to be revolutionary. Naturally, Bitcoin, the very first application of what is now called blockchain, having yet reached the scale of other payment systems such as PayPal, Alipay or WeChat Pay, has fallen short of many people's expectations. In fact, many people do not view Bitcoin itself as an application of blockchain but a blockchain on its own, and its function as a financial instrument is but the innate transaction capability of the blockchain. For a blockchain application worthy of the name, many believe that it has to be built on blockchains such as Bitcoin with functionalities and use experience similar in category and appearance to those of the mainstream applications such as our social media apps. However, this is a misperception on the nature of blockchain born out of using the old Internet mindset to understand the new Internet based on blockchain.

The primary goal of a blockchain is to store data in a secure and immutable way. These data are commonly known as the transactions in the network. The key here is that a transaction can be anything, as long as it can be sent through the network, and the fact that the network has a native currency, Bitcoin, means that each transaction can be marked with a certain value. What sets the Bitcoin blockchain network apart from the existing, predominant Internet infrastructure is lies precisely in the fact that the Bitcoin blockchain is inherently a value network, as indicated by the title of Bitcoin's original whitepaper: A Peer-to-Peer Electronic Cash System. In other words, the invention of blockchain denotes an underlying instrument for value transfer, which means that as long as value exists and is transferable by means of the network, the application of the network is fulfilled. Whether or not it carries with it the ability to support other applications to be built on top of it is a matter of scaling and commercialization. Although the effort to achieve such goals is currently underway and could significantly boost the value of the individual blockchain network, it should not be confused with the definition of the blockchain itself. In this sense, critics have created a false promise that Bitcoin and blockchain themselves did not include in its original design.

However, it is equally important to point out that what the critics often refer to as the failure to create blockchain-based apps is, to the delight of many, gradually being overwritten by a group of emerging blockchain startups. These companies intend to apply the concept of crypto-economics from mining as proof of work to secure a blockchain network to other areas, the most promising of which is social media, an industry plagued by user exploitation and poor data privacy protection. While the critics only saw blockchain as a technology to secure financial assets, they failed to recognize the implications of applying such security guarantees to other fields.

Perhaps the most palpable misjudgment that the blockchain and Bitcoin critics made is that they overestimated the confidence that the public as a whole see in the sovereign economic systems and thereby underestimated the market for the use of cryptocurrencies and their underlying value. Although the characterization of cryptocurrencies as a challenger to the sovereign currency systems is questionable, there is little doubt that that Bitcoin as a decentralized, central-bank-less digital currency has established itself as a secure, trustworthy instrument to store wealth in a way that is largely unfettered by the economic ripples of the sovereign economic systems, especially considering it was created in the midst of the one of the worst global economic recessions of the post-gold-standard era. The value of it, therefore, derives from the market's distrust

27

of capitalism's innate tendency to self-destruct and the need for an alternative monetary system which is not at the mercy of a particular state.

When looking closely at the support and the enthusiasm that Bitcoin generates among its tens of millions of supporters around the world, one would discover that, in fact, the market for such alternative monetary system is quite sizable on a global scale. Thus, when asked the question what makes Bitcoin and other cryptocurrencies valuable, the answer comes quite easily: because there is a large group of people who trust the Bitcoin system. In a post-gold-standard world where the value of a currency is no longer dependent upon its gold reserve, the sway of public trust makes or breaks an economic system more easily. Overlooking this factor is the reason why claims such as Bitcoin is "probably rat poison squared" are incomprehensive in its assessment of the technology to say the least.

Moving one notch deeper into the criticism that cryptocurrency is not trustworthy is the moderate claim that although Bitcoin and others are secure to a degree due to its decentralized nature, the trust that they provide would still not be as appealing as the trust standards guaranteed by a central bank. Consequently, cryptocurrency's trust is really just an illusion created masked under short-living technologist zeal. This is the claim best demonstrated in a 2018 Intelligence Squared Debate titled "Bitcoin is More Than a Bubble and Here To Say."[2] However, as more countries began to examine and adopt blockchain solutions as an enhancement of trust to their financial systems, this claim is defeated by itself. The self-defeat of this argument lies in a slippery human bias that "what is working must be working forever" or "what works means it cannot be improved." That is, although the public generally tend to place their trust in the hands of their central bank, there are many issues with it that have led to the economic malaise in recent memory in many countries. Hyperinflation and high-friction global transactions are the common examples. Coincidentally, mechanisms in cryptocurrency can effectively address these issues.

However, cryptocurrency skeptics often ignore the complimentary benefits that the technology brings to the existing systems too much to realize that the existing systems would adopt the new technology themselves. One may simply call them "too enthusiastic in their conservatism to be conservative."

The history of technological transformation is rife with antagonistic thinking, usually dividing people into two camps. One camp believes in that new technology should be embraced because we have no choice, as even if there are flaws to the technology, the best way to address it is to develop it fast enough to cope with the damage. Fundamentally, this camp believes that technology is essentially good for the world. On the other camp, people believe that technology should be curbed in how much it permeates into society. They may not state thus literally, but they mean it, by and large, in consequence.

Many in the latter camp believe that the alternative monetary system provided by cryptocurrencies would amount to a challenge to the state-led sovereign currencies and therefore would be not tolerated by government regulators. There is some evidence that points to this direction (in the U.S. in particular), but there is little doubt that the concerns of the government are not on the clarity of the benefit the new technology would bring to society but on the regulatability of the new technology. Some regulators are hesitant about the technology because they see practical difficulties in implementing oversight over something that is decentralized. Who is to be held accountable becomes a real question.

However, the difficulty to do so should not be confused with a lack of will from both the government side and the business side. At least both the government and the innovators acknowledge that we have to understand the technology since it is already here. Luckily, escapism only constitutes a very minority in the regulation committees of various governments. The fact that cryptocurrency is a new technology requires effort to be made by businesses to lead its innovation and the from the government to provide more regulatory certainty to enable such innovation. Hindering regulatory processes is detrimental to progress (although some politicians have no qualms in stating explicitly that they are indeed anti-innovation). One can easily make the case that without the innovation of Bitcoin, many of innovative government-driven blockchain initiatives would not have occurred.

In an interview with Dr. Craig S. Wright, the creator of Bitcoin, in China, he said, "Bitcoin has always been about regulation. Many people don't understand this point. The concept of Bitcoin is that it is a publicly accessible and traceable ledger. This is how it stops money-laundering and other illegal activities." [3] If we recognize that Bitcoin's history is blemished with imperfections, we must also see this history as one of progress. Progress and flaws exist in conflict as well as in harmony. In this sense, innovation and regulation happen in congruence necessarily, for mutual benefit.

ONE

THE INTERNATIONAL RACE IN CRYPTOCURRENCY

July 17th, 2019. U.S. Capitol.

It was business as usual for most people in the room. But somehow to the world outside, the hearing felt more solemn and significant than a dozen of other meetings that take place in the building every month. Members of Congress scattered along the four long rows situated on ascending stairs. Situated in the middle of the third row was a big podium, the seat for the Chair of the United States House Committee on Financial Services. In front of the committee, on the lower level of the floor, sat a smaller long desk, behind which sat only one person. Grey haired with glasses on, he was David Marcus, former president of PayPal and the head of Facebook Messenger. He was about to enter a 6-hour-long hearing to testify before Congress for something completely different from social media - money: digital money.

This venture into digital money would be a sequel to Facebook's earlier efforts to incorporate transaction capabilities into its platform. However, this time, the political stir and the public resistance were palpable. Facebook, after its Cambridge Analytica and the Russian election interference scandal, had decided to add to its plate another gigantic, global project, despite public boycott and celebrities deleting their accounts on the platform, damaged reputation, as well as slumped stock price of this tech giant. Bringing its tainted reputation to a new venture seemed uncalled for, especially into a sensitive area that is money. One could only imagine in a situation like this, no matter how significant the technology was, public and governmental resistance would just be the least of their problems. Regardless, Facebook had decided not only to launch a global transaction platform, but a digital currency, the governance of which the company would be a part of.

If one wants to understand why a social media, ad-selling, 2-billion-user tech company would want to endeavor into money, you must look at the competitors across the pond in a different country - no, not the U.K. - China, the home to the world's largest mobile Internet population.

AN UNEXPECTED CHINESE RIVAL

The short history of China's recent Internet platforms is marked by its rapidity of development. When Facebook took off in 2005, China's social media space was still in its fledgling stage. It was after several Chinese university students copied Facebook and started their own social media network for university students in China. With the popularization of Internet use in the country, the Chinese social media network grew quickly to catch up with its U.S. counterparts. However, unlike Facebook, Chinese tech entrepreneurs didn't end there. In October 2010, a project called "WeChat" began at a research center in the city of Guangzhou under Tencent, one of China's largest Internet company. With new features and easy-to-use interface, one year after launch, WeChat reached 100 million users, becoming one of the fastest-growing apps in China. Coincidentally, WeChat and Facebook's Messenger app shared the same year of birth in 2011. But in 2014, WeChat made a decisive move that would prove to be visionary and would make it outpace its American peer.

The Chinese culture has an old tradition of exchanging packets of money among friends and relatives during the Chinese New Year Festival. These packets are also called red envelopes for its red color, symbolizing luck and joy. Based on this tradition, during the Chinese New

Year in 2014, WeChat introduced a feature for sending digital red envelopes between users. With a promotion campaign during China Central Television's most heavily watched New Year's Gala, WeChat's red envelopes quickly gained steam. 16 million red envelopes were sent in the first 24 hours after the launch of this feature. Bundled together with this feature was the requirement that users must be a WeChat Pay user first. In the month after the Chinese New Year, WeChat Pay's user base grew from 30 million to 100 million.

An interesting fact is that at the time of the explosive growth of WeChat Pay, another platform was already dominating the online payment space - Alipay, a digital payment platform under Jack Ma's Alibaba Group. Most people never expected that a new peer-to-peer payment platform could take root under the shadow of Alipay. It hence was a surprise to Jack Ma when WeChat combined the social network and the payment function, creating a competitor in a model unseen before.

It turned out that social and payment were an ingenious combination that is very cohesive for the users: in 2017, with 600 million active users in WeChat Pay, it took over Alipay as the leading digital payment platform in China. People used it to pay for utility bills, book doctor appointment, purchase flight tickets, order food, buy movie tickets, call for taxi, and a variety of other services. Because of WeChat Pay, WeChat became what was called a "mega-app" - an app that improves efficiency in every aspect of your life. From large transactions to smalls ones conducted at small street food vendors, WeChat Pay would replace cash as the preferred payment method. For the millions of the unbanked population in China, WeChat Pay finished the job of banks within in a decade. In 2018, WeChat surpassed 1 billion monthly active users. Whereas plastic credit cards are still used in the U.S. and most western countries for everyday payment, because of WeChat Pay, China became literally "cashless" and "cardless". Together with Alipay, these two payment platforms completed a highly efficient Chinese digital payment infrastructure.

Western investors and tech observers would eventually pick up the news of China becoming a cashless society long after the fact. It is indeed counter-intuitive to hear that the U.S., where PayPal had existed for about two decades, would be outpaced by another country in updating its financial infrastructure, where the use of credit cards is still dominant. Also, domestically, it makes one wonder what kind of effort and how much time it would take to make mobile financial payment the norm in the U.S., where it is still more common to see card swipes in shops despite many alternative, more convenient solutions. It seems that as long as credit card fees keep generating service fees for the banks, a completely mobile-based payment platform will stay years from the making. Factors like these have blinded the industry observers in the U.S. from the rapid deployment of cashless payment platforms of Chinese competitors in the digital payment space.

By the time American companies had realized the scale of digital payment system in China, the country had successfully spread the mobile Internet to both cities and rural areas. In 2018, $414 billion worth of transactions were made through mobile payment platforms in China, 28 times from five years before [1]. In contrast, 2018 saw $64 billion spent on mobile transaction in the U.S., a fraction of the total global consumer spending (roughly $40.5 trillion). In every measure, the U.S. has lagged behind in updating its financial infrastructure into a mobile, cashless basis.

Although WeChat's success is still obscure to many in the U.S., for tech insiders, the benefits of creating mobile payment systems have been demonstrated very clearly in the Chinese market. Businesses now could move around their money faster and shorten their business cycles by processing payments faster than when they were conducting transactions through banks. The Internet companies that built these platforms also were able to generate billions of revenue dollars through various services around the payment platform. At the same time, the competition from these Internet companies encouraged the banks to streamline their services and integrate with the new digital economy.

Seeing the success of WeChat Pay, the U.S. tech platforms decided to do something similar. Although they were not in direct competition against each other, the parallel between the Chinese companies and the American ones does resemble one years earlier, when it was the Chinese that were emulating the U.S. tech scene. How would the American social media giants respond and what kind of approach would they take to build their own mobile payment infrastructure?

LEARNING FROM WECHAT

March 7th, 2019, in response to the heavy public pressure on Facebook's poor privacy record, Mark Zuckerberg published an article titled "A Privacy-Focused Vision for Social Networking," [2] in which he states in addition to the privacy encryption features, Facebook will "build more ways for people to interact on top of that, including calls, video chats, groups, stories, businesses, payments, commerce, and ultimately a platform for many other kinds of private services." For anyone familiar with the features available on WeChat, it is hard to ignore the resemblance of the vision laid out by Zuckerberg in the article to the existing suite of services available on WeChat. Could it be that Facebook had finally decided to go after what WeChat had started with five years ago?

In 2015, the founder of U.S. tech media *The Information,* Jessica Lessin, wrote an article titled "What Facebook Should Learn from WeChat," [3] in which she dives into how Facebook's Messenger could use the payment feature to attract businesses to grow on the messaging platform. It was suggested that Messenger could have ad promotions for brands and enable a shopping feature for its users, both of which had become a familiar reality by that point for WeChat users. Based on WeChat's experience, these new features would help the Facebook ecosystem enhance user experience and create opportunities and new ways of engaging with customers for small businesses. At that time, both apps had comparable user base: WeChat had 500 million users and Messenger had 600 million. If successful, together with the ecosystem of Facebook, Messenger should be able to achieve a mobile payment platform similar in scale and functionality to that of WeChat and offer such services to the world. From a rational standpoint, it was a great opportunity for Facebook to pursue and expand their business and start to move away from the sole revenue source of selling advertisements. The news had told us the public, however, that it was not the path Facebook pursued. It was only four years later, in 2019, that when facing questions from the government over Facebook's privacy protection mechanisms in its ad-selling business model, did Zuckerberg reveal his regret.

"If only I'd listen to your advice four years ago," Mark Zuckerberg posted on his Facebook right after his article, referring to Lessin's article four years earlier. Exactly which piece of the "advice" he was referring to was unclear, however. Still, it was in little doubt that whether it was business integration strategy or payments, either would have benefited Facebook a great deal and possibly help reduce the damage it had suffered in its reputation. The loss of having failed to learn from its peer, on the other hand, was obvious. By then, WeChat had built a seamless digital life experience, whereas Facebook had got stuck in a public trust crisis. Once again, Facebook had become the one playing catch-up: on one hand, it was trying to get itself out of the privacy scandal; on the other hand, it needed a full range of new services to reinvigorate its advertising-dependent platform. An innovation at this point would not only diversity Facebook's business model but also move its public perception in a new direction. Regardless, it needed something new.

LIBRA

An important question to ask is: since WeChat Pay had pioneered moving currency to its paperless, digital form, how would Facebook accomplish something similar with its more than 2 billion users around the world? In addition, being a global business, what kind of new challenges would

Facebook face? How does it differ from WeChat Pay or Alipay? The answer came in the form of a white paper published on June 18th, 2019, entitled "An Introduction to Libra." Two years in the working, Facebook's initiative to transform the global financial life, aiming to bring what has happened in China to the rest of the world.

By no means is Libra less ambitious than Facebook's original social media initiative. In order to understand the thinking that took place behind the announcement of Libra cryptocurrency, we must understand the problem the project is trying to solve.

From the Libra white paper, we can see one key goal that Libra has: it wants to create a global currency and financial infrastructure that anyone in the world can use. It should sound very similar to Facebook's original mission to create a social network that anyone can use to connect with one another. In other words, Facebook's social network has successfully connected billions of people from around the world socially, and now it is gearing up to connect billions financially.

From emails to search engine, from digital maps to message apps, from photo-sharing to music-sharing, from viral videos to movie streaming, this wave of Internet has created for us an Internet where information can be transferred at virtually no cost. The Internet of information has secured us the ability to access and move information on our fingertips. We have thus grown much smarter compared to our ancestors in the pre-information age. However, we have yet done the same to money. Money right now is still being stored the same way information used to be stored in its physical form – paper money. As much as most people in the world can access the Internet with a cheap mobile phone through a wifi hotspot, with money, most people are still trapped in the stage where laborious transaction processes are needed if cross-bank or cross-border payments are involved. The promise that is the "Internet of money", where people can handle money without friction, is the next stage of Internet development.

Having witnessed the power of the Internet of information, it is hard to overstate the potential of the Internet of money. Humans now are at the dawn of complete informational freedom, what will happen when we have financial freedom as well? Historical lessons should offer us plenty of optimism in terms of the benefits that such financial revolution should bring to the world. Libra seems to be a step in the right direction.

Upon first looks, Libra and WeChat Pay do not differ in a way that immediately catches the eye: WeChat Pay has banked the unbanked in China and its surrounding regional markets successfully, while Libra intends to establish a financial infrastructure to do the same on the global scale, both circumventing the need to involve third-party banking services. It would, therefore, be easy to conclude that the key difference between the two platforms is on the question of geography – that Libra is a global project whereas WeChat has a more regional focus, so far as we can tell. However, although the regulatory hurdles of accomplishing such a feat in both western countries and the rest of the world require a significant amount of resources from the part of Libra – the likes of which no less if not more than the resources Facebook is pouring into its social media platform – the question of geography is ultimately a competition in scale and compliance. Libra's ambition that stands out from the rest of the digital financial market ultimately lies in the structure and the kind of financial platform it is.

On WeChat Pay, the user has their own wallet that accepts the existing fiat currency that all banks use. People can transfer funds from their bank accounts to their WeChat wallet without any friction, and their identity is confirmed through the already stored identity on their WeChat account, thus getting rid of the need for verification from the bank. It is therefore a simple wallet-to-bank relation, and the WeChat financial ecosystem ultimately operates as a part of the larger Chinese financial infrastructure, with its outreach extending to the degree of the national system. However, in contrast, Libra intends to implement its own financial infrastructure independently. Similar to WeChat, Libra will have a digital wallet, named Calibra. But unlike WeChat, the money that comes in and out of Calibra is not the fiat-based digital money that is backed by a sovereign government. Instead, it is a separate digital currency issued on the Libra blockchain, backed by a basket of multinational assets and governed by an independent Libra Association comprised of a hundred different financial corporations. As a result of this independent blockchain-based currency, Libra has created an entirely new type of financial governance entity that almost functions as a pseudo-bank, which, for an outside, can easily be confused as a bank for its capability to issue money. At the same time, because the currency is based on a group of other national currencies, its ability to transfer value from one to another makes the currency itself supersede national sovereignty. That is, a kind of super-sovereign currency – a new global financial order that we have only heard in theory but have never seen in practice.

A NEW GLOBAL ECONOMIC ORDER

The existing currency system dates back to 1944, one year before the end of World War II, and traces to a small town in New Hampshire in the U.S. named Bretton Woods. Politicians from the major allied powers gathered there to discuss reconstructing a post-war global financial order. The resulting monetary management system out of the meeting would then be named "Bretton Woods system."

Regular people these days understand that whatever it happened during the meeting gave rise to the Gold

Standard where the U.S. Dollar became the only currency pegged to golden and other currencies would be pegged to USD. However, this monetary system was only one of the two systems proposed in Bretton Woods. The other would be the "International Clearing Union" proposed by John Maynard Keynes.

John Keynes proposed the establishment of the International Clearing Union to issue a universal "world currency" for multilateral exchange. This would exclude gold as the necessary global reserve and allocate the share of the "world currency" based on the average annual value of imports and exports of the country in the first three years of the war. This plan was ultimately preceded by the USD-centered global system, and the International Clearing Union's role would later be replaced by the International Monetary Fund. However, although history did not choose Keynes' path, the idea of a global currency rang through the past seventy years to today and sees itself in the new global currency, namely, Libra.

History proved Keynes' plan to be the more prescient one, as the announcement of the U.S. President Nixon to abandon the gold standard in 1971 spoke the words of retirement of gold as the global reserve, but still left the U.S. Dollar as the dominant global trade currency.

When fiat money disenthralled itself from the restraints of the gold standard, the U.S. Dollar was blessed with renewed, immense power in the international monetary system: although the U.S. GDP only constituted 24% of the world's economy in 2018, the USD made up 61% of the world's reserve. This imbalance between the economic contribution and the weight the respective currency carries would have a series of negative financial consequences, ranging from high inflation to other inequalities in the distribution of financial resources. The concept of a super-sovereign currency has offered solutions to these structural inequalities.

It is important to mention at this point that super-sovereign currency does exist already in the current world. Euro is a super-sovereign currency based on its predecessors in Germany (mark), France (franc), Spain (peseta), Austria (shilling), and other EU countries. It is therefore important to note that the Euro currency exists in congruence with the sovereignty of these individual nations, not necessarily in conflict. This serves us as a brightening demonstration that Keynes' idea was more than idealism.

About fifty years after the dismantling of the Bretton Woods system, a group of international corporations, namely the Libra Association, took up the never-realized mantle of Keynes to launch the global currency that is Libra. The corporations, unhinged by the ideological restraints and the political obstacles that state governments face, aim to accomplish something sovereign nations have failed to do. The implications of the rekindling of the Keynes' spirit cannot be overstated and can only propel a new round of thinking in the digital payment space and hence a new round of innovation in the global financial sector. Up to this point, months after the launch of this initiative, the challenge that Libra's super-sovereign initiative has mounted to the sovereignty of many nations and central banks can be seen in the various capitals. People have already begun to ask: what is the future role for the sovereign state in the future financial order?

THE INNOVATORS & THE REGULATORS

The essence of currency is trust. Moving forward from the Bretton Woods system and away from the golden standard, we have had a transition from placing the value of the currency in the value of the gold reserve to the backing of a government. The sovereign currencies have been able to enjoy the established trust of the state, which lends the stability and the prosperity of the economy to the value of its currency. The U.S., having been the largest economy in the world since the end of WWII, still has its currency as the number one foreign currency reserve in the world. On the trust issue, there are two groups of people that should be a very high priority for Libra to establish trust with: the government regulators and the billions of its potential users, especially with the more than two billion users on Facebook's various applications. However, convincing the regulators of the value of Libra has so far bore the brunt in Facebook's progress in meeting the regulators.

When we look at the Congressional hearing on that cloudy day in July, it is readily noticeable that the overwhelming majority of the opinion on the Capitol Hill toward Libra falls into the category of skeptical or critical, with support for innovation only representing a small fraction of the state representatives. The question is, therefore, quite counter-intuitive: if Libra's initiative is to build financial infrastructure that would benefit billions of people that banks and governments have failed to cover, what were the grounds on which the U.S. Congress could argue against the push for Libra?

There are a few obvious sources of resistance that the government regulatory body has used to question the legitimacy of Libra's initiative. These include: first Facebook's poor privacy records, Facebook's "dominance" in the social media space; second, Facebook's self-practiced political censorship; and third, The concentration of power within the Facebook management structure; and 4. The legitimacy of a monetary system owned by a corporate entity, rather than a state.

The more perceptive audience would have discovered that only one of the above questions actually addresses Libra, with the rest of the questions more or less redirecting to the poor public relation records of one of the many dozens of corporations behind Libra, namely

Facebook. In a sense, looking away from the innovative concepts of Libra but focusing on the less publicly palatable areas of privacy violations is illustrative of the approach taken by the U.S. government: in the short term, more intense regulatory measures need to be put in place in light of the recent user data scandal, but in the long term, financial innovation is still a priority for policy makers, although it might not be as evident so far as the short-term public focus goes.

However, the conclusion from the overall attitude lawmakers in the congress is that the resistance that Libra faces in the U.S. marketplace forebodes possible delays in the use of Libra in the country. For many innovators and from the perspective of technological innovation, using the criticisms against privacy malpractices on a new finance-related product does not help the American market prepare for the potential disruption Libra could cause, especially considering that the resistance is only short-erm

If we want to penetrate the fog of noise around Libra's new technology, the question we need to ask is: when billions of the unbanked population moved to Libra's platform using its financial services, the management of such platform becomes very important - who exactly controls Libra? Upon that question, members of the U.S. Congress launched a series of similar questions to David Marcus, current Head of Libra, during the hearing of House Committee on Financial Services:

"Facebook, which is a publication platform, an advertising network, a personal telecommunications platform, a surveillance corporation, a content distributor, now also wants to establish a currency and act through its wallet as at minimum a payment processor? Why should these activities be consolidated under one corporation?" - Congresswoman Alexandria Ocasio-Cortez, representative of New York's 14th district.

"Of the members [of the Libra Association] today, how many did [Facebook] hand select?" – Congressman Anthony Gonzalez, representative of Ohio's 16th district.

"By what criteria were the initial members of the [Libra] Association chosen?" - Congresswoman Nydia M. Velazquez, representative of New York's 7th district.

"If you think of [Libra Association] as a bank in the sense of a central authority, the idea of the Libra Association could ever become decentralized, I think, gives a lot of people a pause." - Congressman Warren Davidson, representative of Ohio's 8th district.

"I don't think any currency should be launched by a non-government entity and should be left to democratically accountable institutions." - Congresswoman Carolyn B. Maloney, representative of New York's 12th district.

The questions above point to the legitimacy of the governance body that maintains and grows the Libra network - the Libra Association. Will it gain the trust of the public? Or even more interesting, should it have the trust of the public? In the words of Congresswoman Alexandria Ocasio-Cortez, currency should be a "public good," while the corporate nature of Libra is elusive on whether currency would retain its current status. The central issue on the subject of Libra is, therefore, how to establish transparent public oversight in the management of the Libra currency rather than end up in an elitist corporate model, over which the aftermath of the user data scandal still looms.

Several features of the Libra project bear the response to the concerns of the government policy makers. All of these features are a product of the blockchain-based solution, the key among which is the establishment of a decentralized governance structure. In a blockchain, a number of validator nodes are required for the operations of the network. For Libra, the responsibilities of these validators include managing the Libra currency reserve pool, maintaining and updating the Libra protocol, and growing the Libra ecosystem, similar to the role of a central bank in the management of a sovereign currency. However, unlike the central bank, the Libra Association intends to have two separate stages defined by distinct ways of managing the network.

The first stage is a permissioned stage, in which members of the Libra Association will have to meet the joining criteria to be a part of the group, one of these criteria being a 10-million-dollar investment in the Libra network. Due to the minimum investment requirement, in

51

this stage, usually it is the established large corporations that have the opportunity. The list of existing members includes investment firms such as Andreessen Horowitz and Union Square Ventures, digital payment platforms such as Mastercard and PayPal, cryptocurrency exchanges such as Coinbase, and various established tech companies such as Spotify, Facebook and Lyft. While this group of high-profile corporations could bring valuable resources to the launch and popularization of Libra, the closed-off system which does not admit public investors would be detrimental to the network's public trust.

However, in the second stage of Libra, about five years after its initial launch, the Libra Association plans to open up the network and make it permissionless, meaning that regular consumers would be eligible to join the association and participate in governing the Libra Blockchain. By Libra's fifth anniversary, it plans to have 20 percent of its voting power in the hands Libra holders based on the amount of Libra tokens held by them. This stage is similar to the shareholder model in corporations, where the largest shareholders and the largest risk-takers have the voting power. Although, from the current technical standpoint of scalability, achieving such an open ecosystem would be very difficult, its new vision of a new global financial system deserves serious discussions.

In the world of currency governance, the Libra model is one of the more open ecosystems compared to most of the sovereign currency governance entities. For example, most officials in central banks of sovereign states are not elected, but appointed by the head of their government, the decision-making committee within the central bank is usually confined to a small group of individuals, and the term duration of each of these officials is usually very long, many lasting more than a decade. A blockchain-based currency governance model, on the other hand, offers more public competition and decentralization of power. The number of validator nodes in the governance entity usually reaches more than a hundred. The passage of changes to the network also requires a 51% majority among the validator nodes. New nodes can be added to the governance entity if they increase their stakes in the network by increasing their token holdings, and existing governing nodes can lose their member position if their stakes are reduced or are overtaken by competitors. If implemented successfully, the permissionless stage of Libra could offer more fairness and transparency to the global Internet currency than many sovereign currencies. In a nutshell, Libra is less decentralized than Bitcoin, but more decentralized than central banks.

While this may sound refreshing to many who believe that a distribution of control to multiple participants in such a financial platform would enhance inclusion of different opinions in a traditionally closed-off space of finance, such distributed design would present many unprecedented regulatory hurdles to the government in establishing public oversight. Despite the high-profile efforts by congressional and senatorial lawmakers in the U.S. to investigate Facebook's executives, it remains unclear how the Libra Association would be regulated given the approximate one hundred governance members and publicly accessible membership. Does that mean the government would have to assemble all one hundred members to the table or that each in-coming governance member would need to provide proof of compliance to regulators before being officially sworn in by the Libra Association? While the latter possibility would seem to defy every sense of the goal of decentralization, the former sounds like a bureaucratic nightmare that doesn't guarantee result. With no precedent on regulating a decentralized network, it remains a big question on what type of regulatory framework would be applied on the Libra Association. Furthermore, the question of how Libra would comply with the more stringent user data laws in Europe exists besides the challenges in the U.S.

Another challenge that Libra presents to the government is that it can easily be considered a threat to the existing central banking system. While digital payment predecessors such as Alibaba and WeChat Pay integrated the existing fiat-based system, Libra, being a currency in itself, is proposing an alternative to the central bank fiat option. While different national currencies are competing against each other in international finance and we are seeing a dedollarization movement represented by a group of regional organizations, the rise of the Libra coin could potentially hasten that process and disrupt the existing sovereign currency dominance as a whole. Ultimately, it would be likened to the expansion of what WeChat Pay and Alipay have achieved in China to the rest of the world. If Libra successfully attracts a variety of payment services, the future of payment could eliminate the need for people to switch between platforms for different purchases and at different stores. The popularization of Libra could be fast and comprehensive, reaching wherever there is Internet access. In that respect, if sovereign currencies do not offer equivalent services, in the retail market, the role of central banks could end up being eaten away by the growing business that Libra cryptocurrency supports and resorting to the multi-currency framework adopted by Libra, or even having its currency completely abandoned by users in countries with a weak central banking system. However, it is also difficult to see how central banks and the government would let Libra expand without a very specific financial framework.

These are just some of the challenges that arose out of the decentralized blockchain technology that current regulators are try hard to grapple with. Another topic concerning the debate lies in the cryptocurrency nature of Libra.

CRYPTOCURRENCY OR SECURITY?

Libra claims to be a cryptocurrency – it inherits the cryptography essence from the original Bitcoin whitepaper, namely, the Internet of Money. However, it differs from Bitcoin in that the value of the currency is derived from the different source.

According to the Libra white paper, the Libra currency is backed by a pool of currencies and assets on a one-to-one ratio, meaning that for each Libra coin, there is an equivalent amount of external assets backing its value. It is what is called a "stablecoin" scenario, where each piece of digital currency is backed by an equivalent amount of external asset to stabilize the value of the digital currency.

Many stablecoins have been in circulation in the cryptocurrency market for some time. The Hong Kong based Tether Limited is the company behind a well-known stablecoin called Tether (USDT). A more recent stablecoin release comes from the U.S. based Gemini exchange by the Winklevoss brothers called Gemini Dollar (GUSD). These crypto stablecoins have served as hedging tools for cryptocurrency traders for market volatility and an onramp for new cryptocurrency users to enter the crypto space, hence creating a demand for these stablecoins. For the investors of the stablecoin, they profit from the dividend that they will receive at the issuance of new stablecoins when demand rises. The Libra currency is likely to be the same.

Therein lies the fundamental difference between the stablecoins such as Libra and cryptocurrencies like Bitcoin: despite the fact that Bitcoin and Libra are both super-sovereign digital currencies, Libra is still based on world's existing monetary system. This makes Libra look more like a security than a cryptocurrency, which would then subject it to the financial laws in the locale of its operation. Either way, fundamentally, Libra would be affected by the underlying economic structure. The basket of currencies which act as the reserves for Libra would eventually have to develop a special relation with Libra to sustain a balance of power between the central banks and the Libra Association, which would yield very complicated geopolitical implications.

THREE COMPETITORS

Since the inception of Bitcoin, there have been continuous debates over the challenge of unregulated cryptocurrencies to the sovereign currency. However, it is important to know that despite all of the controversies, no country has so far explicitly banned the use of Bitcoin. Many state authorities have arrested illegal actors in the space associated with investment scams and account frauds, as well as money laundering and the use of cryptocurrencies in exchange for illegal drugs. Even China, which much of the western media depicts as a hostile actor toward cryptocurrencies, contrary to public knowledge, has only banned Initial Coin Offering activities due to prevalence of scams. In many countries, even Bitcoin ATMs have been in legal use. This, in fact, is quite contrary to how many Internet startups saw their growth in its early stage. The most notable example was Napster, which amassed 80 million users in its short life span of about two years before a government shutdown. Therefore, actually, the trajectory of the cryptocurrency development has mostly faced an unopposed government attitude to say the least.

In a technology age, the worst consequence from a new technology for any government is that one particular winner from another country takes everything. The fear of "winner takes all" – the competition between state actors – forces them to embrace innovation. From the perspective of the state, it is crucial to lead in the technological front.

In the cryptocurrency space, there are three important state and super-state actors. We have learned from earlier that China has led in the mobile payment front by a huge margin compared to the rest of the world, and their system still remains vastly superior compared to the primitive applications from blockchain. On the opposite side of China is the U.S., which is rapidly wrapping up its mobile payment infrastructure through companies like Apple and Google. The third actor is Europe, specifically the U.K., which is very new to the cryptocurrency payment space. All of the three actors want to be the first to implement a new global financial system, and the cost of not starting it now is extremely high, geopolitically and financially.

China

2019 marked two major pushes made by the official Chinese authorities in the blockchain and cryptocurrency area. The first is the official emphasis on the development of blockchain technology by the Chinese president Xi Jinping during a Political Bureau group study session at the end of October. He stated that blockchain should be an "important core technology innovation breakthrough window" and encouraged "accelerating pushing blockchain technology and industry innovation development." [4]

Almost concurrent with Xi's speech was a more detailed speech by the Vice Chairman of the Executive Council of China Center for International Economic Exchanges (CCIEE), Qifan Huang, during the first Bund Summit in Shanghai organized by China Finance 40 Forum (CF40), a think tank consisted of the highest level of financial expertise in China. During the speech, Huang pointed out that DCEP (Digital Currency Electronic Payment), the cryptocurrency initiative headed by People's Bank of China (PBoC), would replace the currency system of M0 (or narrow money) and greatly help the circulation

of the Chinese Yuan internationally and reduce the
dependence on the current international transaction systems
led by the United States, namely SWIFT and CHIPS. [5]
From these signals, we can see the global ambition behind
the Chinese effort in the cryptocurrency space.

As a side note, the ambition of China calls for itself
as a result of China's rising economic status and its
discrepancy with the voice that China has in the decade-old
global financial establishment. For example, of all of the
cross-border transactions, 41% is taken up by SWIFT [6];
and 43% of global foreign currency exchange belongs to
BIS (Bank for International Settlements). An alternative
system could help the country in its international trade and
may prove to be rather appealing to many other countries
who see that a new system provides them with more
opportunities.

However, thinking that the Chinese strategy stops
short of DCEP would be mistaken still. China's central
bank, PBoC, in fact, started studying and researching
blockchain and cryptocurrency as early as 2015. In 2016,
the blockchain technology, was included in the 13th Five-
Year Plan, which is the primary economy development
initiative in China. These years have seen a maturing
market in the country with a booming blockchain research
and business scene. In this regard, China has an
internationally competitive domestic market force.

Another breakthrough in blockchain for China in 2019 was the passage of the Cryptography Law that outlines the legalities the use of cryptography technologies in the country. In the law, one can see a heavy emphasis on the popularization of cryptography-based technologies, which means that the blockchain companies in China would soon have a much higher regulatory certainty to run their business on. Although many specific details remain the same, such as the legal status of ICO activities and cryptocurrency exchanges, the role of cryptocurrency and blockchain has been confirmed by the law. China's blockchain research and commercialization, from now on, should only be more and more substantial in the international space. At the same time, we can expect a potential integration between the current mobile payment infrastructure, a centralized system, to a blockchain-based system, decentralized.

China has long become the world's second largest economy, but the status of its currency has not risen to the same level globally. Currently, it is seeking to strengthen the use of the Chinese Yuan on a global scale and has successfully done so with many countries and through different projects. The key for using blockchain for the Chinese is to carve out a new financial framework that reflects the success of its economy, and, so far, we have seen little competition to it on the international front. With the openness of Chinese existing financial infrastructure, we can reasonably expect an ecosystem built on top of the blockchain-based solution, similar in scale and popularity to that on WeChat Pay and Alipay. The real challenge is, if China really wants to take a step further from where it is now, it should seek ways to include foreign countries in the mass use of its new system, both on the state-to-state level and on the civilian level. This would require a higher level of openness in its plan.

The U.S.

When it comes the U.S., one important factor on how welcoming the attitude of the U.S. regulators and finance experts is rests upon the fact that fifty per cent of Libra's reserve basket is the U.S. Dollar. With a large portion of the reserve in the U.S. Dollar, Libra ultimately is a convenient tool for the boosting of the U.S. Dollar as the dominant global currency for transaction settlement.

One important stakeholder in all this is the Federal Reserve of the U.S., an entity that is more authoritative in the finance space compared to the divided congress. In September 2019, the chairman of the Federal Reserve of the U.S. Jerome Powell gave words of encouragement publicly to the proposed stablecoin of Libra. He said, "We do want to see responsible financial innovation. We think that's key. We think that will enable people to be better served and drive costs out of the system so it's important that we be open to that." [7]

The words from Powell are in stark contrast to the dismissive attitude of many of the congressional representatives. However, Powell's emphasis on "financial innovation" spells out the readiness of the U.S. currency side to work with the Libra project team. It is, hence, not a far stretch to infer that, with such will for cooperation, the short-term concerns in the Congress and the Senate would remain "short term," and these concerns would mostly relate to money-laundering, terrorist use, drug purchases, and etc., which are separate issues from the focus at hand.

Overall, we can conclude with some confidence that the current attitude adopted by the top U.S. finance minds is one of cautious encouragement. For the short-term political turmoil, Powell's appeasing words went as: With Facebook's very large network of more than a couple billion people, a stablecoin could be systemically important very quickly if it were to have wide adoption. That's not a foregone conclusion, but because of that, we would think that Libra would need to be held to the highest standards. In short, "the highest standards" should not halt progress.

Albeit the optimism we can give to the development of Libra from the perspective of the U.S. state, Libra's reserve composition is exposed to serious risks precisely because of its concentrated ties to the U.S. currency, the kind of ties in which currency instabilities of one side puts the other at significant risks.

Perhaps the greatest weakness in the design of Libra's reserve pool is that although the value of the Libra cryptocurrency is backed by legal assets at the ratio of one to one, it is comparatively a rather low ratio: compared to the seven to one ratio of Hong Kong Monetary Authority, for example, which has 450 trillion U.S. dollars for its currency base. In addition, without regulatory laws put in place, Libra's exchange with fiat currency could easily be taken advantage and used as arbitrage tools by powerful speculative forces, as seen in many currency manipulation cases that we have witnessed in the past decades. This would require additional financial resources for the Libra system.

In other words, on one hand, Libra fundamentally does not leave the realm of traditional methods of creating a currency, in that it derives its value from fiat money, a model which has inherent stability risks. On the other hand. Libra is ground-breaking for its vision to connect the world financially through the power of the Internet, which is faced with unprecedented technical challenges and regulatory uncertainty. In competition with other new financial systems based on similar technologies from other countries, the mild support from the state would not amount to become a significant booster in the short run. However, in the long run, if provided with adequate regulatory and protection, it could usher in a new era for both global finance and regional transactions.

The U.K.

With heightened participation from both China and the U.S., blockchain-based financial systems have entered rapid growth in the past few years. The imperative of the technology has become obvious for many countries, including the U.K., the country which, having irreversibly lost its dominant economic status since the end of WWII, has an unparalleled understanding on the protection of its national interest and what new times mean for their financial system.

Governor of the Bank of England, Mark Joseph Carney, in his annual Mansion House speech, began by saying that "There's a new economy emerging driven by changes in technology, demographics and the environment." Then he moved on to state the imperative to upgrade the U.K. financial system to the standards of the digital era, "This new economy requires a new finance." [8]

In the plan of the Bank of England to rebuild its financial system is a well-founded understanding on areas of the U.K. financial infrastructure that is lagging behind compared to other countries. A decade ago, the Faster Payment System (FPS) was launched to facilitate direct interbank transfers and has hence reduced the payment processing speed to within two hours. However, this system is having a hard time keeping up with country's growing digital economy, with a quarter of its retail sales happening online. At this point, the FPS system is still unable to power in-store or online purchases, as the necessary software systems have yet to exist. In contrast, not only is the U.K. lagging behind China and the U.S., countries like Sweden, India, and the Netherlands have all either launched or adopted some form of digital payment technology that offers superior services to what is available in the U.K.

In addition, the existing systems in the U.K. are high in cost. Currently, the popular UK card payments charge between 0.5% and 2% of the total transaction value for each transaction, not to mention its slow processing speed.

Facing these challenges, Bank of England brought up the idea of launching a cryptocurrency as early as 2016. Victoria Cleland, then Chief Cashier and currently Executive Director for Banking, Payments and Innovation of BoE, stated that the rise of third-party payments, P2P transactions, and public fundraising had brought significant changes to the British economy and that BoE must undertake efforts to rise up to those changes. One of the efforts is a "central bank-issued currency (CBDC)," which could provide "extending access to central bank money" to businesses and households. [9]

This, in fact, is one of the earliest state-backed attempts in researching into the feasibility of using distributed-ledger technology to establish a new financial system for business use. It undercuts stateless cryptocurrencies in terms of regulatory legitimacy and offers transaction protection at the trust of the central bank.

A project like CBDC would give the central bank of the U.K. two advantages:

- The central bank would have the capacity to offer a viable alternative to the unregulated Bitcoin and establish oversight in the cryptocurrency space.

- Businesses and consumers would benefit from having direct access to the central bank without commercial banks as intermediates.

Bank of England would ultimately decide to move the digital currency initiative to the hands of the private sector and focus on rebuilding its Real Time Gross Settlement (RTGS) system. It would opt to back the fiat-based digital currency initiatives from non-central-bank entities and conduct trials before expanding the scope of availability. Nonetheless, the goals of these adjustments remain the same. In Governor Carney's 2019 speech, "the RTGS rebuild will … now provide API access to users to read and write payments data, as well as implementing a system whereby each payment will be tagged with information in a standardized format across the world." From just a few years back, when the central banking system was only accessible through the commercial banking level, such opening-up was unprecedented and should reliably "speed up settlement both domestically and across borders."

To take a step further, Carney also expressed further plans to open up the central bank's access to new payment providers which propose to issue tokenized assets through blockchain, enhancing the business application, and tech companies which plan to issue an international stablecoin, such as Libra, enhancing the retail side. Regulations aside, this welcoming gesture opens up profound doors for banks and tech companies and creates a huge upside for the U.K. in the digital currency landscape.

In December 2019, the U.K.-based company Saga, boasting an advisory board that includes finance masterminds such as Nobel laureate Myron Scholes and J.P. Morgan's Jacob Frenkel, launched its sage (SGA) token, a digital currency backed by a basket of fiat currencies that form the International Monetary Fund's special drawing rights (SDR). This basket differs slightly from Libra's reserve, as it includes euro, Chinese yuan, Japanese yen and British pound, offering a less American-centric finance pool.

This is exactly the type of platforms that would enhance the retail capabilities of the U.K. financial system, and one notable fact is that it was started by a U.K.-based firm. The opening of such platform gives a strong indication that the effort by BoE has created an attractive environment for financial innovation.

On the side note, there are many more differences that set Saga apart from Libra:

- The Saga company will not be profiting from the platform, as opposed to the profit model in Libra consortium, which can be an advantage for the company in terms of regulatory compliance

- SGA tokens will be launched on cryptocurrency exchanges and available for purchase, which will give the token a first-mover advantage in the market, although its resilience and mass adoption fronts would remain contested, as it does not have Facebook's swaths of users

- The firm will not build its own digital wallet like what Facebook plans to do with the Calibra wallet, suggesting that the project is a more open system, both in the regulatory sense and more assuring in the user privacy protection sense.

From the example of Saga, we have started to see the growing competition and enriching ecosystem in the sovereign currency-based fiat currency space.

From the British effort, we observe a focus on accelerating the popularization of digital payment system that modernizes the economy that has differences and commonalities with what we have seen in the U.S. and China. As a differentiating factor, the central bank has adopted a more-welcoming gesture toward financial innovation from the private sector, although it does not mean that the regulatory framework would be any less stringent. However, similar to China, as a country which does not hold the world's most dominant currency, enforcing such innovative ideas helps it reduce its dependence on the U.S. Dollar and facilitates financial independence. Also, with a focus on fiat-based cryptocurrency, we can form a reasonable argument that fiat-based currency is currently the most feasible choice for the next financial system.

Review

The challenge that super-national cryptocurrencies present to the sovereign fiat currencies form the bulk of the existing debates around the future of cryptocurrencies. The first decade of the existence of this new money did not see an explosive growth of its usage or its derivative applications, mostly because of the illegal activities that are associated with its use and an unproductive public perception campaign that failed to convince people of its value. However, features of immutability and openness were picked up by state-level bankers to improve the financial infrastructure of the national level. The concept of a cryptocurrency became the source of inspirations for many central banks around the world in solving the issues in the civilian-level digital transaction capabilities to improve the country's financial efficiency and make the economy more competitive. At the same time, governments in different countries also realized that the new technology of blockchain could be the foundation for the next generation of the global financial system, opening up a new frontier for international financial competition and a race to become the first in creating such system.

The U.S. effort to create a new financial platform globally is led by a global tech firm that has marred public records and faces often hostile government oversight, but that does not seem to hamper the company to continue to make progress in its technology. In fact, the marred public records give the company plenty of incentive to break through the public resistance and create a new business model through the new system that it is creating. Furthermore, it is actually more difficult to see how the tech firm would not utilize its huge platform and exhaust all possible maneuvers to make its cryptocurrency project a reality, as the return on such effort is astronomically profitable. To aid the effort of the company, a minority of sympathetic government policymakers see the matter from a global-competitive standpoint, namely, the competition in creating an efficient financial platform from Europe and, particularly, China. These government officials see plenty of reasons for the U.S. to actively support the establishment of such financial platform so that it would be one which is in favor of the U.S. interest, considering that overseas competitors have already built financial payment systems bigger and more efficient than what is available in the U.S. These forces occupy a minority, although hugely influential, part of the U.S. government. The delicate situation presented to the U.S. is, therefore, although technically conflicted, confused domestic audience within the country.

This presents a political disadvantage for the U.S. compared to some other countries where the government is determined to develop a cryptocurrency to upgrade its financial infrastructure. However, that is not to say that the U.S. is at a disadvantage in terms of technical capabilities. Based on the progress Libra has made so far (mostly through its Facebook team), the Libra network could have the capacity to support a user base on the hundred-million level. Within five years, according to Chinese sources, networks such as Libra could support a base of up to one billion users. [10] This further consolidates the point that the hurdles of Libra and other American projects mostly lie in the regulatory aspect.

One particular area of development for Libra to mention is Europe, however, where a picture of success for the project could stay indefinite for an indefinite time. Mainly, what differs Europe from the other infrastructure-hungry regions in other parts of the world is regulatory and geopolitical. On the regulatory side, even though the Europeans do not have an attitude as hostile and emotionally charged against the key facilitators of the project as that in the U.S., the regulatory enforcement gives an amount of pressure no less than the pressure from the U.S., if not more. Based on the strictness of Europe's cyber-related laws, we can expect that the Europeans are more concerned with the regulatory compliance of the project and the protection of the rights of its citizens than a speedy commercialization. From the geopolitical standpoint, we see that there is not as much financial incentive to be eager to support a USD-heavy project as in the U.S, especially given that some countries in Europe have already a digital payment platform working well for its economy. These differences present another layer in the international success that the Libra team hopes to see.

China and the U.K. enjoy a relatively more supportive government attitude, which paves a smoother path for the advancement of their blockchain effort and explains the quick development of the technology in these two countries. Both countries see an urgent necessity to apply blockchain in its financial infrastructure, although for different reasons and different in the stage of development.

China displays a more developed scene both in terms of the current level of financial infrastructure maturity and its technical capabilities. Its current plan proposes a grand domestic ambition to completely replace cash with digital currency, issued by the central bank to commercial banks and then to the hands of people. It can be considered an upgrade at most in its almost cashless society. On the technical side, China's capacity to support a large user base on blockchain is very competitive with what the U.S. offers. Jingtum Tech, a blockchain firm based in Beijing, which started developing its blockchain back in 2014, can already support a mass commercial user base of ten million, moving toward 100 million in 2020. It also possesses a multi-layer blockchain bottom layer and cross-chain capabilities, the only one in the world. In contrast, Libra's network does not have shards or a multilayered architecture in its technology. By mid-December in 2019, Jingtum Tech had achieved a commercial user base of two million and a transaction capacity of 5000 transactions per second (TPS), [11] and Jingtum is just one of several examples that China's early-mover advantage has given rise to.

The real challenge of China's blockchain initiatives lies in its international ambition, namely, establishing an alternative to the existing international financial systems controlled by the West, chiefly the U.S. In seeking such approach, China inevitably needs to develop closer ties politically and financially with its neighboring countries in a region that is withstanding geopolitical uncertainties that are not necessarily conducive to such developments. However, seeing the preliminary welcoming gesture from many countries in the Eurasian landmass toward the China's One-Belt-One-Road initiative, we can develop an educated guess that the various economy forums that have been founded in the region - be it ASEAN, Shanghai Cooperation Organization, or certain participants of the APEC - could foster an regional environment that could see the success of an alternative international financial system in the long term. In this sense, although China faces certain political challenges, due to the success of existing initiatives and different geopolitical forces at play in the region, an internationalization process for regional financial infrastructure could gain a lot more momentum in many countries initially compared to Libra.

The reason for the U.K., to expand its digital payment infrastructure, on the other hand, is more domestic than international. Although creating some international digital currency based on multiple fiat currencies could bolster the role the British financial system plays in the world, the urgency for such project arose from the discrepancy between an increasingly digitalized economy and an increasingly outdated payment system for its citizens. We henceforth saw the "open door" policy that Bank of England adopted in encouraging third-party players to innovate and create a more accessible payment system for businesses and consumers. From this policy, we have witnessed a growing number of interested corporate parties to offer their proposals. In this sense, therefore, cooperation and regulatory compliance come before political disagreements and international competition, which we see more heavily in other countries.

The implications of this standpoint come in twofold. First, the U.K. could fast-track its digitalization of its financial system with its open-door policies; and second, multiple different systems would want to build a bridge between their infrastructure and the U.K.'s. Geopolitically, this is a well-balanced approach, considering that the country has witnesses initiatives from other major players take off, and it is consistent with the neutrality that the U.K. has adopted in many international topics.

Overall, cryptocurrency offers a completely new model for countries to globalize its financial system, and this in turn also will have a wave of further changes in macroeconomics. The U.S. has the technical capabilities and resources to quickly implement its project, but is mired in regulatory uncertainty; the U.K. is opening its doors to quickly digitalize its economy but effect is yet to be seen; and China, which has both the technical capability and the early-mover advantage in digital payment, has its fiat-based M0 cryptocurrency in the horizon but has not revealed its international roadmap. What makes this scenario a unique case is that not one country has the sole dominance in the technology, and therefore time is of utmost essence, in that whichever country is able to construct such a system that is safe and receives international support, this country will start to enjoy the benefits of the system early. For mutual benefits, cooperation is key in this space, but there will be no shortage of competition either.

BITCOIN IN THE CONTEXT OF REGULATION

While Libra's head David Marcus was sitting through the six-hour hearing answering questions from dozens of lawmakers in Washington, the cryptocurrency community came under a profound revelation: ten years into the existence of Bitcoin, the government has failed to and probably will continue to fail to exert a central governing power over the "digital gold" that is Bitcoin.

For the past ten years, Bitcoin has been able to enjoy a period of little government intervention in terms of its growth and use. The several instances where government crackdowns and regulatory hearings happened were Bitcoin-related businesses such as cryptocurrency exchanges and platforms that supported the use of Bitcoin as payment. Without a central authority leading the Bitcoin project, the government cannot pinpoint one particular point of contact to regulate, not to mention to call upon to attend a hearing. Numerous previous attempts to identify the individual or individuals behind the pseudonym "Satoshi Nakamoto" have only resulted in failure and publicity ridicule. Regardless, even if the real-life figure behind Satoshi came under public spotlight, there would still lack a solution to shut down the whole network anyway through the creator, as from the moment he published the network to the hands of the public, the network became forever under the management of the public. At most, the government can be a participant in the network, but no more.

Furthermore, Bitcoin does not require any government consent at all to establish its utility as a payment tool. As long as a user has a Bitcoin wallet, they can send and receive Bitcoin. Even if one country completely bans all Bitcoin activities such as mining, trading and even technical development, community members in other countries can pick up the baton and carry on. None of these would endanger the Bitcoins that are in the wallets of the users. "No single point of failure", a core feature of decentralization, applies to every aspect of Bitcoin. In this sense, the creator of Bitcoin, Satoshi Nakamoto could take pride in building a decentralized network no one could break and smirk at Libra being asphyxiated by lawmakers in the cradle.

However, there's a crucial difference in the definition of "decentralization" between the Libra project and Bitcoin. Although Libra also claims to be decentralized, it is heavily different from the way Bitcoin is decentralized. For Libra, the beginning period of the platform requires consistent centralized input from its core leader up to the point when it transitions to a more distributed platform, whence it would achieve a degree of decentralization, which would still be lesser than that of Bitcoin. During the decentralized stage of development, the initial project leader would continue to have significantly diminished control over the Libra network as part of the Libra governing entity, namely the Libra Association. Any changes made to the Libra network must be deliberated and approved through the Libra Association In other words, the power of the network is concentrated in the quasi-decentralized governance body of the Libra Association.

The only similarity Libra shares with Bitcoin in terms of governance exists in the stage of creation: after the initial development phase of Bitcoin, the creator released it to the public and exerted increasingly less influence in the post-release period. However, there is no central governance entity anywhere in the formal structure of Bitcoin. Bitcoin became decentralized in the hands of its miners the moment Satoshi Nakamoto released it to the public. The various developers that contributed to its code base and built on top of the protocol did not need the consent of a central governance body and the changes made are decided on its acceptability by the large group of nodes in the network. To characterize the contrast between the different degrees of decentralization between Libra and Bitcoin, we can call the decentralization on Bitcoin "decentralized to the individual level" whereas the decentralization on Libra came down only to the "corporate level." Hence, in the eyes of the Bitcoin community members, Libra does not come close to decentralization and is centralized in the hands of a few billion-dollar corporations. In other words, Libra's decentralization is only relative to the system to which it is being compared.

The pros and cons of being largely "unregulatable" in use and development have been debated and made an unavoidable subject as a result of the various organizations that have shown to be leading the direction of the project. On the one hand, many community members stick to the tenet of "decentralization for absolute individual freedom" and champion the path of unregulability of Bitcoin. On the other hand, in order to be accepted in mainstream society, Bitcoin must prove to the government regulator its regulatability so that the decentralized platform does not just become a haven for piracy, drug exchanges, money laundering and speculative activities. The logic here is, if the Bitcoin platform can offer businesses superior services and applications, why can it not be compliant with the law that these same businesses already abide by? Especially since that compliance with the law would enhance public trust in and of itself. In the early stage of Bitcoin, the community was heavily tilted towards the former view, but more recent development has given rise to a group of outstanding organizations in favor of the more moderate approach.

Australian computer scientist Dr. Craig Steven Wright, whom many believe to be on the original team that created Bitcoin (although the subject remains highly controversial), has adopted a pro-business, pro-regulation posture in popularizing Bitcoin. He believes that that Bitcoin, as it is originally intended, inherently takes government into account. Bitcoin's "ability to track and track and trace money, to limit and report on corruption and illegal foreign dealings alters the very nature of government." 12 These are deemed to be the "productive aspects of society oversight" that the government offers. On the other hand, "in a representative society," the public expenditure and capital-raising methods in the government could be monitored and traced through the Bitcoin blockchain. The result would be a more transparent system where "the commons will be controlled and owned, and such members of the district will be able to gain the benefits that come from maintaining a system well, and they will be able to hold them who abuse the system to account." In other words, blockchain is a solution to corruption.

Wright's arguments fling far from the anarchist parts of the cryptocurrency community who believes that cryptocurrency should be censorship-resistant. They argue that there should be no point of central control over a blockchain network that could practice censorship. They also often categorically resist any centralized power in any shape of form, and therefore they often believe that the government has no role in decentralized blockchain networks. This call for anti-censorship and privacy protection in cryptocurrency has led to a number of "privacy coins" which make transactions difficult to trace. However, these projects often have "heads that are visible," meaning that they have key points of power in the network, which exposes the network to the risk of "single point of failure." If one of these points gets taken offline, the survival of whole network is endangered. In addition, although the government may not be permitted as a viable participant in a blockchain network, the central point of power could easily be transferred under a different name, namely the project team that maintains the network. In Wright's words, "the very people making the argument have the power to invalidate transactions." He calls this the "sophistic rhetoric."

A truly pro-business, pro-adoption blockchain should not ignore or underestimate the role that regulation and the government play in the processes of new technologies. Neither should it seek to avoid it. Dealt well, areas of initial conflict could give rise to valuable opportunities. In fact, if planned strategically, new technologies could be the engine for improvement in government processes and create opportunities for adoption and business. The traceable feature of the Bitcoin blockchain is a great testament to the saying that government and new technologies do not need to go head-to-head.

BITCOIN & THE FUTURE OF FINANCE

2015 was the turning point for the global economy, where an economic recession started to move in the direction of an economic depression. The whole world started accentuating supply-side reforms. In 2016, China started to emphasize financial stability and stabilize its much hyped-up real estate economy, and many countries around the world continued to sell more and more American debts. In 2017, the U.S. entered a period of raising interest rate. In 2018, Sino-American trade conflicts phased into being. In 2019, the Chinese real estate market witnesses its point of reverse, and the global population witnesses its point of reverse, namely decline. Also, in 2019, the U.S. entered into a period of quantitative easing (shorted as QE). These signals raise an important prediction: the second half of 2019 could open a global economic depression, reaching a historic low in the global market in 2021.

Currently, the anchor of the U.S. Dollar, since the break-away from the Bretton-Woods System in 1970, has been oil. More and more so, countries have departed from a USD-centric financial system back toward the gold-centric system to stabilize their own currencies.

In essence, gold still remains the primary anchor for currencies around the world, for its involatile physical traits and preservability, rarity, relative consistent total quantities, and most importantly, a global recognition. It is also an asset in which the U.S. does not have monopoly.

The U.S. has successfully, by the end of the 20th century and in the beginning of the 21st century, controlled or effectively put under its influence the key oil-producing countries. The result is global financial on the U.S. currency when countries needed oil. However, when fall in the oil price combines with overprinting of American dollars, countries would revert back to gold to move away from the American system. Without its anchor of the oil, the American currency loses its value.

The American Dollar needs a new anchor, and Bitcoin is the only viable candidate for it.

Although the Washington policymakers may not want to admit it, and would continue to have a hard time to accept, Bitcoin these days possess three key characteristics:

- It has a rapidly growing global consensus, from a digital toy ten years ago to a global digital currency with a user base of 40 million. It is not a far fetch to estimate its user network reach multi-hundred-million in the next decade.

- It has fixed total quantity of 21 million coins, decided by the set-in-stone algorithm from the start. No artificial intervention could change it.

- It has a decentralized distribution of its wealth. So far, 18 million coins of the total 21 million have been mined, with the rest 3 million to be mined in the next 100 years, and there are only 15% of the total value are in the control of "whale" holders.

In essence, the Bitcoin market these days is a decentralized one in every sense of the word, be it in terms of mining, possession or fiat on-ramp. The largest point of competition will be on the control of fiat on-ramps. Whoever controls them will have the power on the cryptocurrency market equivalent the power the Ottoman Empire had on the East-West trade.

2018 saw an explosive growth in the state support for cryptocurrency. Compliance exchanges such as Bakkt are a signal of that. The next logical step is the establishment of a set of regulatory framework and laws that set the standards for "Digital Gold as a Reserve Asset." [13] Granted, the timeline of this next step is uncertain, and the speculative nature of the value of the current digital gold, namely Bitcoin, remains an obstacle to, but the various advantages of a digital value reserve asset to the transparency of a financial system have laid the groundwork for such digital transformation of value, just like how information went digital during the Internet Boom, to occur.

Hence, the future of finance will likely be one in which many state digital currencies and public-blockchain-based decentralized cryptocurrencies with broad public consensus like Bitcoin.

TWO

CHINA'S BLOCKCHAIN DETERMINATION

China, as we have discussed with a degree of depth in the previous chapter, occupies a leading role in the innovation of blockchain technology. It recognizes that blockchain is a powerful innovation like the internet and massively pushes its blockchain initiatives. This has created a peculiar phenomenon: China has successfully integrated the economic advantages of technological innovation and the political goals of consolidation of state power. In fact, the rapid speed at which blockchain application and research move forward in China gives a compelling testament to the efficiency of the state power. Whereas most people would think that blockchain, for its decentralized nature, would be a tool that necessarily entails decentralization in power and wealth from the ground up, it equally creates valuable opportunities for established institutions to innovate and solve problems from the top down. At the most basic level, blockchain is not just a playground for private initiatives such as Libra, but also an arena where government of state modernizes itself to suit the need of the new age. In this chapter, we examine how the state can play a driving force, instead of a limiting force in blockchain innovation, particularly in the Chinese context.

BLOCKCHAIN IN THE CONTEXT OF THE CHINESE NOTION OF STATE

As we have seen in the first chapter, the Chinese state has so far played a deterministic role in the development and the popularization of the blockchain technology. On one hand, it has banned the trading and the public fundraising activities surrounding cryptocurrency. On the other hand, the blockchain technology has been given a top priority in the technological goals set by the Chinese central government. We can identify from this ambivalent attitude toward the product of the technology and the underlying technology itself some clarity as to the role that blockchain has been assigned to in China.

Firstly, given a de facto race between China and other western countries on technology, China has viewed blockchain as a strategic technology to advance to fulfill its goal of increasing technological independence rather than a reliance on western technologies, either software or hardware, which has been the dominant picture over the past four decades; secondly, China sees blockchain technologies as a strategic economic opportunity to elevate its financial standing in the global economy while providing an alternative international financial system to itself and other countries which would welcome it; and thirdly, for its domestic economic scene, China views blockchain as a further step in its pursuit of building a state-of-the-art, efficient digital economy, and in turn making the Chinese economy more competitive globally. There is also some debate over the extent to which blockchain will be used in the government across different levels to curb corruption and make it a more transparent, efficient governance system, but the evidence remains chiefly economic. So, primarily, there is one technological benefit and two economic benefits from the development of blockchain. And what we can observe from these focuses is that the Chinese state is applying a decentralized technology quite coherently in its centralized system. In other words, the Chinese government, in its adoption of the technology, does not see a contradiction in the structural level between how the government is organized and how the technology is applied. In fact, the Chinese government arguably sees that the decentralized aspects of blockchain a tool of high potential to improve the efficiency of its government processes. Such is the Chinese mindset behind their embracing of new technologies. And since it has been made a state mandate that China needs to be the leader in multiple technologies, as stated in China's strategic plan of "Made in China 2025," the use of technologies such as blockchain and the example it sets has significant implications in how China approaches other technologies in transforming its society. To understand this, we need to understand the larger picture of the role the Chinese state gives itself in the traditional and modern Chinese civilization.

THE ORIGIN OF THE MODERN CHINESE STATE

In this part, we attempt to understand the role that the Chinese state plays in the development of China and the role that the relationship between the Chinese state and new technology, by taking a historical approach which would provide insights into the role that the Chinese state has traditionally taken upon itself and the ways that technology has been viewed as a tool for the development of China and the stability of the state. Through this historic approach, we attempt to build a framework with several key points for the understanding of the modern context. Then in the second part, we put the current circumstances of the Chinese state in relation to new technologies such as blockchain in light of the framework we developed. The goal is to provide the contemporary audience that is interested in the direction that China is taking with the development of various technologies, such that the public in the West at large has a tool in understanding the Chinese tech scene in face of the its opacity to the non-Chinese world.

The first key element of the Chinese state throughout its antiquity and its modern times is unity. Ancient China, specifically the Spring and Autumn and Warring States periods, and medieval Europe shared a common history of a multistate system, where in both cases, the feudal system existed as the dominant governance model. However, the divergence in their political history appeared as the various Chinese warring lords transformed their domains into sovereign states with a centralized administration, and the multistate system became a contest of strength between the different centralized systems across these different states.

Ultimately, the strongest of them all, the state of Qin dominated the rest and started the history of a unified Middle Kingdom.

The feudal system continued in Europe well into the 15th century, while the centralized administration of Qin, guided by the legalist ideology, ended feudalism in China at the point of its founding in late 3rd century BC. Since, up to the end last dynasty of the imperial China, the Qing Dynasty, in the early 20th century, China had developed a cycle of the rise and fall of Chinese imperial states, all, however, under a centralized administration that maintained the unity of China. The individual European states, in contrast, gradually developed various systems of check and balance that governed their individual states without forming a unified European system with a centralized governance entity.

The key characteristic of the imperial China is that, although a centralized administration existed in all of the dynasties and remained mostly unchanged as its sole political system, an internal cycle of replacement of administrations appeared as the successor to the previous failed administration to continue the unity of China. This thus becomes a theme in the historical unity of China, characterized by government which had failed to maintain the stability and order of the unified Chinese society would be succeeded by a new government, until a new government was needed. Therefore, throughout the more than two thousand years of the imperial Chinese rule, emperors would study the failures of previous dynasties and develop mechanisms for resilience for the lasting of their own government. This is evident in the longevity of the individual dynasties throughout ancient China: whereas the first unified dynasty of Qin only lasted fifteen years, later dynasties would last up to four hundred years (although it seems that as no dynasty lasted more than that, there is a theoretical limit on the longevity of the Chinese imperial system).

While in the Chinese political history, a pattern of order and disorder, or toppling and renewal, is readily observed, the European political system also seems to be subject to such a cyclic pattern, although for structural reasons: the ruling emperor was ousted for disrupting the system of checks and balances, rather than necessarily replaced by newly founded revolutionary government, and a new emperor would be installed in place of their ousted predecessor. Therefore, the historic contrast between the cyclic patterns in early modern Europe and imperial China seems to suggest that while European systems would offer the political structure the freedom to continue its current governing body by selecting out the disobedient element, the Chinese history has the proclivity to replace such a governing body in its totality for a new one until further replacement is required. In more technical terms, historically, the evolution of political system in Europe had been intra-structural, whereas such process in China had been inter-structural.

Therefore, if a new government was to be installed in China, its imperative would be nothing other than developing a resilient system for social rule that would survive the test of time, or even better, a system that would self-evolve during the transitional times of calls for a different government.

Following the historical perspective, however, we must be careful in arguing that the modern Chinese state is a logical continuation of imperial China – one of the reasons being that the imperial China had a weak sense of modern national identity. That having been said, the historic lens can help withdrawing parallels between the modern Chinese state and the imperial Chinese system and help us see the historic influences inherited from the imperial period into the modern Chinese system. One important area that we will put specific focus on is the responsibility of the state in the pre-modern and modern period and, in the context of that period, we can briefly figure out where the source of legitimacy for the Chinese government comes from.

The first observation we can make about the fall of China's imperial system and its transition to a modern nation-state is that similar to all other dynasties in the cyclic dynastic pattern, the last of the Chinese dynasties, Qing, failed to deliver on the what is called "the Mandate of the Heaven," which means the blessing given by the Chinese people to its ruler in exchange for the prosperity and the stability of the nation. By the end of the 20th century, the Chinese Empire had been carved up by western imperialism and encroachment of its long-standing East Asian neighbor, Japan, and had since devolved into a half-colonized, half-feudal state. This awkward position, in which the Qing government retained its sovereignty but was handicapped in the exercise of its state power by foreign imperialist presence, left China to search for a way to revitalize its national sovereignty to compete with the invaders while maintaining its traditions in state affairs. By the end of the Qing government in 1912, however, the weakening state of the Qing government had been so severe and reforms so slow, that internal forces in China rose up and created a new government to advance the goals of "Revitalization of China." The responsibility to restore the national sovereignty of China and to build a modern, industrialized China fell onto the shoulders of the republic government.

Although the Confucian traditions and "the Mandate of the Heaven" had been replaced by the democratic values and socialist policies, and the establishment of the republic government in 1912 meant that China had finally ended its imperial history and became a modern nation-state in name, the western infringement of its national sovereignty remained and that its industry, economy, as well as the sense of being a part of a Chinese state on the civilian level stayed weak. When the Japanese invasion of China started in mid to late 1930s, China had to counter that invading force in addition to its anti-colonial effort that had been on-going in the pre-invasion period. By the end of the World War II, the republic government, despite consistent aid and military supplies from western allies, had been mired in hyperinflation, and the long-promised land reforms and other socialist policies were never realized due to entrenched elite interest. Having suffered continuous defeats in the Chinese theater from Japan and sabotaged industry and agriculture, China remained in a feeble position where it is economically stunted, militarily weak, and politically unwieldy by the end of the war. In other words, the thirty years of the republic role had not delivered the promise of "reviving China."

Although it will remain forever in mystery whether or not the republic government would eventually be able to carry out the policies it set out to in mainland China, the Chinese communists drove them out to Taiwan and established their own government in 1949 to continue their own style of land reforms, industrialization, and economic growth. With the enormous success of the Chinese Communist Party government in its first 5-Year Plan and its strategic success in repelling the United Nations forces back to what is now the Military Demarcation Line, the

Chinese achieved a degree of success, for the first time in decades, in protecting its national sovereignty and improving its national infrastructure. After the war, the Chinese repossessed Lushun Naval Base and Chinese Eastern Railroad. With ensuing successes in further strengthening its sovereignty several border conflicts and its rise in the international stage, despite domestic turmoil in the 60s and 70s, China never had to face foreign aggression in its home territory, the significance of such achievement can be viewed in comparison to the many other struggles for independence in other previously colonized parts of the world. In other words, the sovereignty part of the China's revival had been achieved with relative success.

During a press conference held by the State Council Information Office of China in mid-January 2020, the head of the National Bureau of Statistics of China stated that the per capita GDP of China broke through the $10,000 mark, for the first time, in the year of 2019. Although in the continuous growth of the Chinese economy, this was well expected, the speed at which China accomplished it was unprecedented. According to the World Bank, upper middle-income economies are those between $3,996 and $12,375. It took South Korea thirteen years to reach the $10,000 mark from the lower $3,996 limit; fifteen years for Singapore, forty years for Brazil, but only twelve years for China [1]. Another significance of this milestone is that the first phase of growth for the Chinese economy is closing to a point of end, where structural economic reforms are needed to deliver the further growth and prevent China from calling into the "middle-income trap." Among the many social and economic challenges that exist in China, preventing China from the middle-income pitfall that many other developing countries have fallen into is the key to accomplishing the next stage of China's revival. According to the Report of the Thirteenth National Congress of the Community Party of China, by mid-21st century, China's goal is to reach a per capita income of mid-level developed countries [2]. The primacy of this goal was then further heightened in the Eighteenth National Congress of the Community Party of China in 2012: China will establish a wealthy, strong, democratic, civil, and harmonious socialist modern state after the hundred years since the founding of the People's Republic. Therefore, it suffices to say that the Chinese government has long had the understanding that he continuation of its existence relies heavily on its ability to deliver during this stage of development. It also understands that this stage of development will be the hardest for China: this period will be a test to its system of governance, its political economy, its demographic change, and its relations vis-à-vis the rest of the world.

CHINESE COMPETENCY

To escape the Middle-Income Trap, time is of essence for China. A former senior director for Asia in President Barack Obama's National Security Council, Evan Medeiros, said in 2017 that China only had "about five years" to become a high-income country [3], which places 2022 as the time for China to reach a per capita GDP of $12,235. We may have two ways to look at the China's plan to avert the middle-income question.

First, if we take Medeiros' deadline of 2022 as the benchmark with which we assess China's results, we may find the current growth rate of China insufficient: with IMF's prediction on Chinese economy's growth rate adjusted to 6% in the beginning of 2020 after the signing of the phase-one trade deal between the U.S. and China [4], China would surpass the $12,235 level by 2022 only if it could deliver a ten percent annual growth rate in the period between 2020 and 2022. This view considers the China's drop from double-digit growth to single-digit growth a fatal loss of steam as it entered into mid-2010s and therefore proposes that China would likely to fall into the middle-income trap like its predecessors. In addition, this view deems the continuation of the state control in China's political economy as an impediment to the further market liberalization that is seen as a necessity to China's continued growth. It argues that Xi Jinping's ideas about the economy, based off the Marxist-Leninist ideology, are not prepared for the political sacrifices needed by a full embrace of market economy to the extent of the U.S. It, therefore, proposes that such "conflict between marketization and state control in China" would prevent sufficient growth in productivity to surpass the many economic challenges.

However, a second approach to answer China's future of growth would focus less on the political structure but more on transformation needed in its economic structure. More specifically, the innovative abilities of the Chinese manufacturers and further liberalization of China's financial sector. China's role in global manufacturing has been a well-known fact: 27 percent of China's overall national output comes from its manufacturing, which makes up 20 percent of the total global manufacturing output, bigger than the portion of the U.S. [5]. However, the magnitude of China's manufacturing industry does not speak to its problems. According to a 2018 paper [6], China's manufacturing faces problems including, inefficient unit labor output, a lack of industry standard, low innovative capacity, low added value but high pollution, and inadequate digital infrastructure. For China, a good student of history, establishing its role as the major global manufacturing hub is a historic necessity if it wants to become an economically prosperous China, like the Great Britain did in the 19th century and the U.S. in the 20th century. In face of these challenges, the Chinese government proposed an ambitious ten-year strategic program in 2015: Made in China 2025. In it, it outlines four transformations needed in China's manufacturing industry: away from element-driven to innovation-driven, away from low-cost competition to quality-benefit competition, away from high-pollution production to "green" production, and finally, away from production-based manufacturing to service-based manufacturing. These four focuses aim to jump-start China's future-oriented, high-tech manufacturing while gradually cutting its high-environmental-cost, low-quality industries, as the country shifts from a quantity-growth model to a quality-growth model. In terms of which industries would best reflect the future progress of human society, China selected ten domains in which it aims to become a leader in [7]:

1. New-generation information technologies such as integrated circuits, 5G, and Internet of Things (IoT);
2. Machine tools and robots;
3. Aviation and space flight technologies;
4. Marine engineering technologies;
5. Railway transportation equipment;
6. Renewable-energy automobiles;
7. Electric equipment such as hydroelectric dams, nuclear power technology, high-temperature superconducting materials and etc.;
8. Agriculture equipment for informationalizing its agricultural industry;

9. New materials; and

10. Biological pharmaceutical and high-performance medical equipment;

Since the inception of the 2025 program, in many regards, China has become a global leader. China's high-speed rail system is the most extensive system of the sort in the world and has scored contracts in numerous overseas markets. In areas of artificial intelligence also, China had surpassed the U.S. in 2015 in terms of the number of AI patents. In 2018, China filed more than 30,000 public patent in various AI fields [8]. Specifically, China has a lead in fields such as natural language processing, data searches, and e-commerce, all high-tech hotspots where major global tech companies have been pouring massive amounts of resources in development. In the more nascent field of blockchain, China's advantage looks even more salient, with a dominance of over 60 percent of the global total number of blockchain patents filed through the period of 2009 through 2018 [9]. In the field of robotics, China has had most industrial robots since 2016 [10]. The explosive growth in these fields come is largely thanks to the increasingly large amount of R&D spending that China has sustained in the past years, scoring a continuous double-digit growth and ranking only second to the U.S. total R&D spending [11]. Even with its current progress, however, we may have only seen the beginning of China's potential. The R&D spending constituted 2.18 percent of China's total GDP in the year 2018 and about 2.5 percent in the year 2019, well below the level in the U.S., Japan, South Korea, and Germany [12]. The result of this focus on the tech-driving manufacturing has been that China is gradually transforming from a labor-based manufacturing model based off its sheer population size to an innovation-driven manufacturing model based off the sheer size of its talent pool. And by making good use of its talent resources, China aims to break the myth that "Made in China" is not innovative and is of low quality. In this regard, China's future lies in innovative manufacturing, in which lies in its industrialization, in which lies its modernization.

On the future of China's financial sector, a brief note can be made as to the potential of China's further capitalization of its market to address the point made earlier on the uncertain future of China's liberalization of its economy. It is a widely recognized reality that with a financial sector worth of $44 trillion in 2018, a retail banking market of 1.1 billion adults and a projected asset pool under management of $14 trillion in 2022 [14], China is not a market that international financial institutions can afford to overlook. It was until recently that despite the promises that China had made over the years since its joining WTO in 2001, real progress of the Chinese market liberalization had not been delivered to the degree as promised, and systemic limitations posed on foreign firms by Chinese regulatory institutions still relatively strict. However, a demonstration of genuine willingness to further financial liberalization in China was seen in 2018, when the China Banking and Insurance Regulatory Commission (CBIRC) was formed from the separated banking and insurance regulators. Since, China has announced and implemented a series of "opening-up" policies in its financial sectors across various areas, including banking, securities, wealth and asset management, and insurance, allowing an unprecedented level of access to the Chinese market for foreign firms [14]. In mid 2019, CBIRC gave the liberalization effort a deeper push with the announcement of its 11-point liberalization measures with regard to China's financial market. These measures span from improving the transparency of China's financial sector, to removing caps on company share of foreign investors, and to opening up whole new areas for foreign investment [15]. The effect on the market shares was almost immediate, to name one example alone: as of April 2019, the overall market share of foreign insurance companies in China had a 1.78% increase in terms of premium compared to the previous year [16].

A liberalization effort of this scale raises many questions on the symbiotic relationship between the Chinese government and the Chinese economy. Although the on-going strategies do demonstrate a political will to deepen economic reform, exactly how much the Chinese government is willing to pursue the liberal market and what would China's political economy look like going down the road of liberalization still remain subjects in question. In addition, it is still worth debating whether a liberalization of the economy in China stands entirely at odds with the political system and the power structure. The new wealth generated by the private sector and the government initiatives taken by the state-own sector sometimes complement each other, as in the new markets where the private firms would not see immediate short-term profit, the state enterprises could act as the initial investors not for immediate returns, but for strategic importance which could benefit private businesses later. Such strategy is well embodied in the Belt and Road Initiative.

The bottom line is, as in the case of China, that economic growth and political stability should go in tandem in the current stage of China's development on course to achieve its hundred-year goals. Unbeknown to many China outsiders, the source of caution and proactivity with which the Chinese government pursues its economic development both come from the lessons offered by recent economic history, namely the collapse of the Soviet Union and the startling inequity and the consequent political volatility in the U.S., the former being an example of underwhelming caution in the pursuit of liberalization and the latter being the example of overwhelming proactivity.

This paradoxical mindset thus explains mixture of contradictions that have been emblematic of nearly all Chinese conduct, in China's internal political activity, foreign relations, economic development, and technological pursuit.

THREE

THE 4-BILLION-DOLLAR EXPERIMENT

After a decade of interest, development, and innovation, the blockchain industry has coalesced into two primary sources of drive: government-backed development as expounded in previous chapters and the private-firm projects. While the government-backed projects often are imbued with political agenda and strategic national interest, private-firm projects generally proceed with such a goal, and such a goal only, to maximizes the number of people who use them. Such projects of an entrepreneurial nature, although lacking the resources and power of the enforceable government policies, deserve studies done on their implications on the popularization of blockchain technology, for reasons that should be well familiar to the contemporary audience – the predominant form of internet platforms we use today unanimously came into being from private initiative. By studying the cases of applications powered by blockchain and the difference in the approach they took in the use of blockchain in different settings, we explore the range of possibilities of what future applications of blockchain might look like, and for many entrepreneurial readers of this book, valuable lessons can be learned from the pitfalls and issues examined in the case.

THE 4-BILLION-DOLLAR PROBLEM

Looking across the top-tier cryptocurrencies in the industry landscape [1], we can divide them into two camps of cryptocurrencies based on their stage of development. The first camp includes Bitcoin, which occupies the top spot in terms of market valuation; Ethereum, which was invented to accommodate applications to be built on blockchain, ranking second in capital market valuation; XRP, the cryptocurrency of the real-time settlement, exchange and remittance network created by Ripple Labs Inc., occupying the third spot; and then the few Bitcoin forks that resemble the original Bitcoin design to different degrees, the most controversial of which being Bitcoin SV (short for Satoshi Vision), which purports to be the original Bitcoin that truly honors the creator's original design. These cryptocurrencies all have a longer history and a better-known standing compared to the rest of the market. Although vastly different in implementation, they all share the same origin of design which is a solution to the prolonged remittance issue in international finance (with the exception of

Ethereum, which was designed for applications). These cryptocurrencies differ from the rest of the market for their time-proven existence and for their simplicity of design in using minimalistic concepts to address a straightforward problem. However, because of their simplicity of design, they are also restricted in the sort of applications they can support. For large-scale, enterprise-level applications, these blockchains do not provide high enough network processing speed. This is known as the scalability problem and has become a defining deficiency of the first wave of blockchains. A low network processing speed would be fatal for an application that has hundreds of millions of users. The higher the transaction speed, the better the user experience is, and the more users are willing to use the app.

This is why solving the scalability problem is so essential for the mass use of the technology. Despite the security it provides, without the capacity to support high transaction volumes, blockchain would not be a realistic platform for building applications. To give an idea on exactly where we are in terms of achieving large-scale processing capacity, *Bitcoin* currently can handle around 4.6 transactions per second, while Ethereum can process three times as much, averaging around 14 transactions per second, both of which, however, are almost comically dwarfed by *Visa*, the long-standing payment tool we use every day, which processes around 1,736 transaction per second, leaving a 37,750% gap ahead of *Bitcoin* [2].

The difficulty of addressing the scalability issue lies in the trade-off between decentralization and speed. With the conventional cloud computing service, data are uploaded and processed at a single-point data center and do not need to travel from server to server until a majority validation by the network. The more servers left to confirm, the more time it takes before majority validation, and the slower the process is. Therefore, on one end of the spectrum, decentralization provides better security as multiple parties guarantee the state of the data, and on the other end of the spectrum, it takes much less time for the data to be processed with a smaller number of parties involved in validation. If tilted too much toward decentralization, the network risks being too sluggish for practical use; and if tilted too much toward scalability, the network risks sacrificing security and other features such as censorship resistance. Striking a balance between the two properties is the challenge [3].

THE 4-BILLION-DOLLAR EXPERIMENT

At the height of 2017 cryptocurrency market bull run [4], a number of "new-generation" [5] blockchain networks designed to address the scalability issues came into being with the promise to usher in mass adoption for the technology. A number of market favorites came about in that period, including Filecoin, which raised $257 million for building a global decentralized file sharing network, Brave, which raised $35 million in 30 seconds for building a free and open-source web browser [6]. However, these projects were towered over by the $4-billion-dollar initial coin offer (ICO) of EOS. From June 26, 2017 to June 1, 2018, Block.One, the company behind the EOS project, ran an initial coin offering (ICO) that raised a total of $4 billion dollars, scoring the largest ICO of all time and the breaking the record as the longest ICO [7]. Unsurprisingly, the EOS project was launched with precisely one goal: build "a highly scalable platform for smart contracts" [8].

To many, $4 billion was a hefty price for a piece of technology. For perspective, the biggest initial public offering (IPO) of 2017 from Snapchat, only raised $3.4 billion. Even within the cryptocurrency space, EOS leads in ICO valuation even farther ahead. This drew some unexpected controversies from the non-tech-savvy media that usually stay off technical topics. A CNBC post titled raised concerns on the fact that Block.One raised the funds "without a live product" [9], and HBO's favorite, John Oliver, opened made fun of the project in a fairly technically dense rant that lasted 25 minutes during his *Last Week Tonight with John Oliver* [10]. Compared with all the other cryptocurrencies in the industry including Bitcoin, it certainly deserves, justifiably or wrongly, to be its own species. The question is: EOS worth $4 billion.

EOS stands out from the rest of the cryptocurrency landscape in several specific ways. The first differentiator is its consensus mechanism, the way in which the network updates itself with new transactions. In previous generations of blockchains, mining had been the model in which a blockchain network reaches a consensus on its transaction ledger through its servers distributed around the world. Computational work is required in this process, and hence Proof of Work is the term that describes the mechanism. However, Proof of Work is computationally expensive and slow as well as environmentally consuming [12]. To replace the expensive and slow computation characteristic of Proof of Work, EOS implements a consensus mechanism that should allow for a much faster network processing speed while guaranteeing a relative degree of robustness of the network. This mechanism is called Delegated Proof of Stake (DPOS).

To get a full picture of the significance of DPOS to the blockchain world, we shall take some time to go back to the trade-offs that underline the design of every blockchain network. This is known as the decentralization-security-speed trichotomy. When we were talking about the scalability issue of previous generations of blockchains earlier, we explained that too much emphasis on decentralization results in slow speed and too much emphasis on speed leads to centralization, and usually security goes with decentralization generally. The question ultimately trickles down to how much decentralization we want without crippling the speed and how much speed we can have without sacrificing decentralization so as to endanger the security and censorship-resistance of a network. These are very important questions for blockchain designers and users and usually are the most heated areas of contention between different camps of blockchain enthusiasts. People who believe that a free internet lies in the utmost degree of decentralization naturally would favor networks like *Bitcoin*, and those who believe that we should be more practical are willing to focus more on speed without cutting too much on decentralization. The designers of EOS understood these trade-offs.

With the self-proclaimed features of "flexible, scalable, and user-friendly" [12], EOS does not shy away from its pros and cons. According to a report by U.S. cryptocurrency investment firm Multicoin Capital, EOS "is designed from the ground up to be scalable, user-friendly, and fast" and the team that designed it "recognizes that decentralization requires tradeoffs in both economics and performance" [13]. What this means in practice is that EOS reduces the number of transaction validators in the network so that it can process transactions faster. Without getting too much into the technical details, EOS has 21 active validators live at a given time from different parts of the world processing transactions and a few dozens more as backup validators for contingencies. These 21 validators are selected by EOS token holders who get to cast votes with their EOS tokens on their preferred "delegates," and by "staking" their votes, token holders vote in the most popular 21 validators to produce blocks as "block producers" (BPs). This ideally distributes the governance of the network into the hands of the token holders and creates a sort of "blockchain democracy", and compared to the concentration of mining power in *Bitcoin*'s and Ethereum's networks, where top 4 miners own more than 50% of the mining power [14], a group of 21 block producers elected through competition for votes could be a quite effective form of decentralization. In other words, instead of the Bitcoin and Ethereum model in which computing power is the ticket to the governance of their respective networks, EOS has a model in which the cryptocurrency itself, a token so to speak, is the vote one needs to govern the network.

Now, there are two questions to ask on the efficacy of this consensus mechanism. The first is how effective is it in achieving the goal of increasing network speed? Second is how effective is this form of "internet democracy?" The answer to the first question is that limiting the number of validators to a set number of 21 has enabled the EOS network to claim a peak speed of 3996 transactions per second, on a par with VISA's speed. However, an independent report in 2018 [15], partly supported by Ethereum-based research organization *ConsenSys*, on the network performance of EOS indicates that due to other components in the network design such as computing resource allocation problems, "during rests with real world conditions," performance dropped below 50 transactions per second, still much higher than that of Bitcoin and Ethereum, but way below what's needed for large scale applications.

Given the fluctuating performance of EOS, it is difficult to reach a verdict on the achievement of EOS. However, one thing is sure, regardless whether it is running at a level near 4,000 transactions per second or at a level closer to 50, such an unstable speed would not be suitable for large scale applications, and it certainly could not support multiple mid-sized to large applications running at the same network concurrently. Ethereum's infamous network congestion was caused by one application in 2017 that had only processed a total value of about $3 million worth of transactions [16]. Considering all the evidence, a safe verdict we can reach might be that a blockchain which balances performance with decentralization would be at most sufficient for one application and but insufficient for more, given a stable performance as a premise. Once we recognize this outcome, we then have a lot of interesting ideas for discussion, particularly regarding the future use of mass adopting blockchain as an enterprise solution. The most interesting implication of this verdict is that the future of blockchain lies in single-chain solutions, meaning that each application shall have its own blockchain and each blockchain can interoperate with others for purposes of information and value exchange [17]. This guarantees that one application could enjoy the full advantages of blockchain while preventing a situation where one application breaks, the whole system breaks.

A DEMOCRATIC INTERNET

When the mass adoption of the Internet began in the 90s, techno-idealists believed that it would be the ultimate democratizer that gives ordinary people more power and dismantles entrenched legacy interests in the government and the media industry. People thought it was the equalizer between the powerful and the voiceless. As it turns out, while having created enormous wealth for society as a whole and given individuals a public forum for discussion, the Internet was ultimately better leveraged by the more equipped, better-staffed, and more resourceful big corporations and governments. While the platform for ordinary people has risen, the big players have risen even higher. Government monitoring is as if not more pervasive on the Internet as it was before. Tech corporations have the ability to censor speech published on their platforms, and they can make such decisions unilaterally in their boardrooms while only subject to often vociferous yet ineffective public pressure. In real-world politics there are still elections that produce democratically elected leaders to govern society, but in the Internet "politics", in its literal sense, decisions are made by technocrats, also literally, and so far as technology regulation is concerns, the elected regulators fall behind the pace of innovation.

This is what makes the governance mechanism of EOS not only refreshing but relevant: with a voting mechanism that allows people to vote in delegates to govern the blockchain, it creates a democracy of a sort of the Internet. The general idea and a key selling point of blockchain is its censorship resistance, and the way to achieve this is decentralizing the governance of the network. For Bitcoin and Ethereum, they decentralize by allowing anyone with enough capital and access to mining hardware to process transactions, and the more capital one has, the more say they have in the state of the network. For EOS, the network decentralizes in a more fundamental way. For the validators in EOS network, although they still need the server infrastructure necessary to support the network, they do not require the expensive mining hardware to participate. In other words, the threshold for entrance is much lower. Furthermore, the top active validators need to be selected by the token holders of the EOS network. This gives the users of the network a certain degree of power to participate in the decision-making of the network. This is accomplished by infusing the cryptocurrency of the network with the utility of voting power (hence such cryptocurrencies are granted the name of "utility token") [18]. When changes to the network such as adjusting the inflation rate of the native token or the voting mechanism are proposed, a certain threshold of votes must be met for the change to pass and come into effect, which brings us to the second important point of the EOS democracy – it is a "semi-direct democracy".

For any changes to the network to pass, a certain threshold of votes must be cast in favor of the policy. These votes come from the general token holders directly. The validators who run the network can cast votes with their tokens too, but their primary function is to implement the changes. This separation of roles bears a resemblance to the separation of legislature and the executive in a democracy, and even as in a real-world democracy, or shall we say "offline democracy," the government policies are not made directly by the voters themselves, but the elected representatives of the people. On EOS, however, the intermediate of elected representatives does not exist, and all the, so to speak, policies are voted on directly by the token holders, which provides several advantages that "offline democracy" does not have. It is fast, it does not have the bureaucratic red tapes of complicated partisan gridlocks, and neither is it constrained by time – it is run online, it is 24/7, and anyone can submit proposals to the community to vote on anytime, and all the canvassing happens online as well. All these, in fact, are exactly why EOS is so exciting to many. The idea of a digital democracy that involves direct participation of its electorates in policymaking without third-party interference that risks corruption seems to be the next step for governments. Thirty years since the mass adoption of the Internet, there seems to be a way to decentralize the power to the masses. Or is it too good to be true?

The EOS governance has several design features that do not have well-rounded scientific backing and therefore are susceptible to human manipulation. The first one is the token-to-vote ratio, set at thirty, meaning that one EOS token could be used to vote thirty times for different block validators. Two sides exist as to the pros and cons of this design. The upside of this ratio is that voters can use their tokens to vote up to thirty of their favorite candidates, but the downside is that since the value of each token is now inflated, the voting power of each token is now no longer linear but exponential. This means that for voters who only hold a small number of tokens, the weight they carry in the system is also small, but once certain people in the system amass a large enough sum of tokens, they can literally monopolistically decide which top 21 block producers are elected. If coordinated well, a cartel of block producers could appear at the top, voting for each and keeping each other in power (known as "mutual voting"). The best example of such is the scandal of Huobi, one of the largest cryptocurrency exchanges in the world and one that runs a EOS block producer node, which came under fire from an internal leak pointing out exactly how many mutual votes have been exchanged between Huobi and its colluders [19].This results in a concentration of power that contradicts the idea of decentralization and has long made the design of one-token-thirty-votes a controversial design.

If the voting ratio is an example of a problematic mechanistic design, then the state of decentralization is worsened by external factors as well. Ideally, EOS tokens should lie in possession of the actual owners, but that is often not the case in the world of cryptocurrencies, where trading activities occupy still a key use of the instrument. For the EOS tokens, a lot of them stay in the wallet addresses of cryptocurrency exchanges that traders have put into for trading. These exchanges hence find themselves in possession of a large sum of tokens that they can use to vote themselves in to one of the top block producer positions in EOS, with the best example of Bitfinex, one of the largest cryptocurrency exchanges in the world, which once had 27 percent of its votes coming from one other voter and the rest from itself and a small group of other sources. The ultimate result is that these exchanges receive further revenue from running the network and continue to expand their influence, and with all the profits going to these top block producers, ordinary voters are disincentivized to vote and distanced from decision-making. In sum, a variety of factors including mechanistic problems and external immaturities have contributed to EOS's "corrupt governance" [20].

To solve block producer collusion and voter disincentive, we might in fact find parallels in democracies in the real world. Voter participation has long been insufficient in many countries, and a few democracies have implemented a compulsory voting scheme to ensure high voter turnouts. Without the enforcement capabilities of nation-state governments, EOS might not find a compulsory scheme feasible for its network, but it could take the route giving benefits to voters for participating in the voting process. If voters can receive a compensation or some form of incentive for voting, they might move some of their tokens out from exchanges to their own wallet addresses for voting.

One such solution that proposes a voter compensation is realized through what is known as "proxy wallets," where voters can stake their tokens and get a rewarded for voting with tokens (proportionately to the amount of their stakes) from the block producers they vote for. The reward, however, comes from the block reward that block producers receive from processing transactions, and the amount is set at a percentage of the block producer's reward by the block producer. That is to say that voters get paid by the block producers they vote for. It incentivizes for token holders to vote and helps many block producers without a big name brand but of high integrity spread their names, but the idea of "vote buying" also makes many uncomfortable. So far, the effect of this solution on the long-term health of the system is too early to tell.

With regard to voter incentive, it is also important to mention another design feature unique to EOS. A blockchain, like cloud computing centers, does not have an unlimited amount of resources for its users. For a limited amount of bandwidth and processing capacity, the network must have a mechanism to decide which transactions get processed. On the Ethereum blockchain, resource management is mediated through the implementation of "Gas," a unit that measures the computation effort that it takes to execute certain operations, such as a transaction, a smart contract and so on. Miners set the price of gas and decides to accept or reject transactions. The higher the gas of a transaction, the more inclined a miner is to process that transaction. On EOS, the network manages its resource allocation through a resource purchase market. In the resource market, the resource of the EOS network are put up for sale priced with the EOS token, which is to say that the resource allocation is mediated through pure free-market mechanisms. Each unit of resource – in this case, RAM, which required to store data on the blockchain– can be purchased by with a certain amount of EOS tokens. Ideally, users who need it would purchase the amount of RAM with some tokens when they need it, and when they no longer need it, they could sell their RAM at current market price. Through this model, the price for the resource is ultimately determined by supply and demand.

The problem with this approach is that the price of RAM is prone to speculation, just like the cryptocurrency itself. Speculative actors could stake large amounts of RAM to heat up its market price and drain up the available resources, in many cases causing the network to be unusable for users who cannot have access to the resources when they need them [21]. However, regardless of these market problems, EOS has found a bona fide role for its token as a measure and mediator for the resource allocation of the network.

Overall, considering the resource market and voting mechanism as a whole, we find an interest fusion of the economic role and the political role in the token of EOS. On the one hand, it is a political tool that determines the governors of the network and carries political value; on the other hand, such political value is made explicitly connected to its economic value. Does this fusion design provide the desirable environment for a decentralized internet? Will it attract more applications to be built on it? In addition, relatedly, what is Block.One, the company that created EOS, going to do with the rest of the four billion dollars?

Fixing Social Media

In 2016, two events with global ramifications took placed that would shock the world. Such events, categorized by mathematician and best-selling author, Nassim Nicholas Taleb, have been widely known as the black swan events. Namely, these are events that are disproportionately high-profile, hard-to-predict, and are that defy normal expectations in science, history and other fields. The two events in 2016 perfectly fit the description and marked humanity's entrance into a new era – the "post-truth" era. The events here referred to are of course the election of Donald J. Trump as the U.S. president and Brexit, both a thunderbolt moment to the established order of our understanding of the society we lived in, and the word "post-truth" was hence declared by Oxford Dictionaries as the international word of 2016. According to Oxford Dictionaries, the definition of "post-truth" is: relating to circumstances in which people respond more to feelings and beliefs than to facts. Since the beginning of the post-truth era, we have seen an emergence of sibling phrases and words such as "alternative facts" and "alt-right" (short for alternative right); it was also since then that we have been visited by the ubiquity of fake news; and it was since that time that people started to understand how intertwined information technology is with politics. The one that wins the information war also wins the political war.

The case to be made about the importance of truth often encounters several challenges. First of all, who gets to determine what is true. Ideally, given facts and evidence, everyone has the cognitive capacity to reach that truth, and such facts and evidence should not just be one-sided, which is to say that when sometimes there are two sides to the story, both sides should be accounted for and considered as reasonable evidence. However, the challenge here also is not to distinguish factually wrong from factually right, but rather dealing with cases in which certain facts are subject to exaggeration for ulterior motives. Hence already, when discussing truths, we are stepping into murky areas.

Although there are all sorts of challenges to the pursuit of truth, it is still a laudable and worthy goal to pursue and respect the truth. Such effort erects a powerful opposition to the blatant disregard for basic fact. That is to say, although reaching the truth is hard, we should all try to at least look for it and respect efforts to do so. There, we may find a solution to our post-truth problems. It is bigger than one individual and requires systemic discipline.

Another piece of the puzzle is, as indicated earlier, the technological piece. The information technology we currently all use in the media space is fertile grounds for sensationalist speeches that appeal to emotions rather than facts, rewarding manipulations of human emotions while leaving the role of facts downplayed. If, ultimately, the proper role of media technology as a tool to promote healthy civil discussions is to be upheld, then certain rules of engagement need to be enforced. The incentive mechanism of the media needs to be overhauled: disregard of facts should have a price, efforts to educate and spread factual knowledge should be rewards, and when disagreements arise, constructive dialogues should be rewards. In theory, these steps forward should appear clear to most people years into the post-truth time, but little change is what we have witnessed in the social media space. Granted, even with all these steps taken, mostly likely there would be dissatisfaction still and perfection is impossible, but if anything, the very fact that the word "post-truth" is characteristic of the world we live in today suggests that there are things wrong in our incentive design.

Could some form of innovative token incentive design help solve the problem? In the EOS governance example we discussed earlier, the economic design of the token is created in a way to incentivize better network behaviors albeit certain flaws. However, it would not be an exaggeration to say that such innovation broadened the frontier of what problems could be solved by new ways of economic design. What kind of system would incentivize factual speech and disincentivize falsehood? It is for this very purpose that Block.One, the company behind EOS, launched its own social media platform called *Voice*.

In the letter to the community by Voice's CEO Salah Zalatimo, titled "Why We're Here" [22], he points out the problems we mentioned earlier of the post-truth era upfront and provided Voice as a solution:

We're living in a post-truth era where many media platforms have lost their way. Media should empower us and bring us together, not confuse and divide us.

Today, our largest media platforms seed fear, uncertainty and doubt into our world. Many of us have thrown up our arms and walked away, deleting accounts and cutting cords in frustration at our disjointed world. Who would have thought in 2020 we would be confronted with questions like: Is this news real? Is this even a human? Is it ok to be racist? Is it ok to break the law?

It's time we started using technology to find a better way.

That's why we are building Voice: a platform architected for integrity, where real people can publish real content and have real discussions. A place where everyone is welcome because everyone respects each other and their right to be different. This is the vision, and we need like-minded people to help us get there. People who feel we deserve an online community free from fake accounts, fake news and fake privacy.

So far early into this experiment, we do not know if Voice's promises will live up to their potential. Privacy and fake news are not just technical problems, but human problems, and it seems likely that the plan Voice has is to design some sort of token incentive mechanism to reward "everyone [who] respects each other and their right to be different." Authenticate accounts with real people's names might be the first step to achieve that, and more disciplined content moderation could be the way to rein in fake news better than the existing social media platforms, and rewards for people who make good points and sound arguments could spark more genuine excahnges. Although time is still needed for any conclusions, it is fair to say that Voice is onto something.

EPILOGUE

A new generation of technology represented by artificial intelligence, quantum information, mobile communications, Internet of thing, and blockchain is accelerating breakthrough applications.

- Xi Jinping, president of China

At the time of the publication of this book, China has launched the testing of its digital RMB in key cities across China before a larger-scale testing among a bigger population. Shenzhen, Suzhou, Xiong'an, and Chengdu are among the first tier of cities to implement the testing of the DCEP system, which is now being used by the public to pay for utilities and a variety of businesses to receive payments from customers. In the smart city of Xiong'an, which is a new metropolis project city run with the latest digital infrastructure, Starbucks, McDonald's, Subway, movie theaters, automated stores, hotels and other businesses have all been a part of the latest DCEP testing. Many people in these cities now send and receive money directly through China's central bank, rather than third-party commercial banks.

Ultimately, exactly what kind of changes a digitalized M0 that is DCEP will bring to society is still uncertain. China's already mature M2 digital payment platforms like Alipay and WeChat Pay have already transformed brought enormous transformations to China's society and economy, but many details about DCEP are still in the making. However, one thing certain about it is that a digitalized M0 is going to further the progress made by a digitalized M2. Obvious benefits of implementing a digital M0 include banking the unbanked in rural China where tens of millions of people still have trouble access banking infrastructure; reducing transaction cost that is still an issue to some on the existing M2 payment systems; increasing asset security and eliminating fraud and terrorist activities in parts of the economy that cannot be regulated with the current system; increasing the efficiency of fiscal policy implementations such as during a recession when the central bank can target specific groups of low-income groups with relief package; and internationalizing China's currency with a more transparent and secure system.

At the same time, criticisms and fears of civil surveillance would arise from increasingly popular national projects. The U.S. with its own national digital currency project would inevitably raise similar fears. But the good news is that there will be a variety of options available to the public by the time large-scale digital economy comes into being. Bitcoin will be a powerful contender when the time comes. Businesses will have the choice of an open system like Bitcoin and less open systems of various national digital currencies. With national digital currencies, businesses will be able to do what they are already able to do at the moment much more efficiently, securely, and at a lower cost. With open systems such as Bitcoin, businesses might invent completely news ways of doing business that are not present in national systems. And the two types of systems do not have to be contradictory, and rather in many settings they can be complementary to each other. Each system will have their own advantages. National systems will enable many innovations within the established systems of different societies to solve problems that have not been able to solve before and give us new data to understand aspects of society previously poorly understood. A currency of the internet, however, that is unrestrained by geography will create a whole new range of possibilities just like the infrastructure itself did.

REFERENCES

BACKGROUND

1. Kim, Tae. "Warren Buffett Says Bitcoin Is 'Probably Rat Poison Squared'." *CNBC*, CNBC, 6 May 2018, www.cnbc.com/2018/05/05/warren-buffett-says-bitcoin-is-probably-rat-poison-squared.html.

2. "习近平在中央政治局第十八次集体学习时强调 把区块链作为核心技术自主创新重要突破口 加快推动区块链技术和产业创新发展." *新华网*, Xinhuanet, 25 Oct. 2019, www.xinhuanet.com/2019-10/25/c_1125153665.htm.

3. De Groot, Juliana. "What Is the General Data Protection Regulation? Understanding & Complying with GDPR Requirements in 2019." *Digital Guardian*, 2 Dec. 2019, digitalguardian.com/blog/what-gdpr-general-data-protection-regulation-understanding-and-complying-gdpr-data-protection.

4. "带着这个特殊身份，黄奇帆出席首届外滩金融峰会." *财经头条*, 大白新闻官微, 29 Oct. 2019, cj.sina.com.cn/articles/view/5996341740/16568e9ec00100ltte.

5. Mougayar, William. "Tokenomics - A Business Guide to Token Usage, Utility and Value." *Medium*, Medium, 6 Aug. 2018, medium.com/@wmougayar/tokenomics-a-business-guide-to-token-usage-utility-and-value-b19242053416.

6. PwC. *Estonia – the Digital Republic Secured by Blockchain.* PwC, 2019.

7. *The Fourth Industrial Revolution* by Klaus Schwab

PRELUDE

1. Stinchcombe, Kai. "Ten Years in, Nobody Has Come up with a Use for Blockchain." *Hacker Noon*, 28 Apr. 2020, hackernoon.com/ten-years-in-nobody-has-come-up-with-a-use-case-for-blockchain-ee98c180100.

2. IntelligenceSquared Debates. "Bitcoin is More Than a Bubble and Here to Stay." *YouTube*, uploaded by IntelligenceSquared Debates, April 23. 2018, www.youtube.com/watch?v=ZceJMFXm57s.

3. "专访 CSW：如果选一个历史人物自比，我选爱迪生." *专访 CSW：如果选一个历史人物自比，我选爱迪生-律动 BlockBeats*, 区块律动 BlockBeats, 9 Dec. 2019, www.theblockbeats.com/news/6342?from=groupmessage.

CHAPTER ONE

1. Rolfe, Alex. "Report: The Future of US Mobile Payments in Numbers." *Payments Cards & Mobile*, 11 June 2019, www.paymentscardsandmobile.com/the-future-of-us-mobile-payments/.

2. Zuckerberg, Mark. "A Privacy-Focused Vision for Social Networking." *A Privacy-Focused Vision for Social Networking*, Facebook, 6 Mar. 2019, www.facebook.com/notes/mark-zuckerberg/a-privacy-focused-vision-for-social-networking/10156700570096634/.

3. Lessin, Jessica E. "What Facebook Should Learn from WeChat." *The Information*, 25 Mar. 2015, www.theinformation.com/articles/What-Facebook-Should-Learn-from-WeChat.

4. "习近平在中央政治局第十八次集体学习时强调 把区块链作为核心技术自主创新重要突破口 加快推动区块链技术和产业创新发展." *新华网*, Xinhuanet, 25 Oct. 2019, www.xinhuanet.com/politics/leaders/2019-10/25/c_1125153665.htm.

5. pi_root. "链博科技：外滩金融峰会上，黄奇帆就区块链讲了什么？." *链博科技*, 19 Nov. 2019, chainboard.io/2019/10/30/链博科技：外滩金融峰会上，黄奇帆就区块链讲了/.

6. [Chinese] Chinese Institute of Digital Assets. *Libra: A Kind of Experiment on Financial Innovation*. pp. 101-102

7. Bloomberg Markets and Finance. "Fed's Powell Says Facebook's Libra Could Become Systemic Quickly." *YouTube*, uploaded by Bloomberg Markets and Finance, Sep 6. 2019, www.youtube.com/watch?v=L1ixjNPDZ4U.

8. Carney, Mark. *Enable, Empower, Ensure: A New Finance for the New Economy*. Bank of England. London, 20 June 2019.

9. Cleland, Victoria. *Fintech: Opportunities for all*. Bank of England. London, 8 September 2016.

10. [Chinese] Chinese Institute of Digital Assets. *Libra: A Kind of Experiment on Financial Innovation*. pp. 39

11. "井通科技." *井通科技*, www.jingtum.com/.

12. Wright, Craig. "Satoshi and the Sophists." *Craig Wright Bitcoin SV Is the Original Bitcoin*, 23 May 2019, craigwright.net/blog/bitcoin-blockchain-tech/satoshi-and-the-sophists/.

CHAPTER TWO

1. "中国人均 GDP 突破 1 万美元，意味着什么？." *中国人均 GDP 突破 1 万美元，意味着什么？*, 中国经济网, 19 Jan. 2020, baijiahao.baidu.com/s?id=1656139038135832461&wfr=spider&for=pc.

2. 胡鞍钢, et al. "2050 中国：以人民为中心的社会主义全面现代化." *中国共产党新闻网*, 国家行政学院学报, 16 Oct. 2017, theory.people.com.cn/n1/2017/1016/c40531-29589477.html.

3. "China May Be Running Out of Time To Escape the Middle-Income Trap." *Asia Society*, asiasociety.org/new-york/china-may-be-running-out-time-escape-middle-income-trap.

4. Carter, John. "China's 2020 Growth Rate Prediction Raised to 6.0 per Cent by IMF." *South China Morning Post*, 17 Feb. 2020, www.scmp.com/economy/global-economy/article/3046890/chinas-2020-growth-rate-prediction-raised-60-cent-imf-after.

5. West, Darrell M., and Christian Lansang. "Global Manufacturing Scorecard: How the US Compares to 18 Other Nations." *Brookings*, Brookings, 10 July 2018, www.brookings.edu/research/global-manufacturing-scorecard-how-the-us-compares-to-18-other-nations/.

6. Feng, L., Zhang, X. & Zhou, K. Current problems in China's manufacturing and countermeasures for industry 4.0. *J Wireless Com Network* **2018,** 90 (2018). https://doi.org/10.1186/s13638-018-1113-6

7. "中国制造 2025." *百度百科*, baike.baidu.com/item/中国制造 2025/16432644?fr=aladdin#reference-[7]-16399676-wrap.

8. Okoshi, Yuki. "China Overtakes US in AI Patent Rankings." *Nikkei Asian Review*, Nikkei Asian Review, 9 Mar. 2019, asia.nikkei.com/Business/Business-trends/China-overtakes-US-in-AI-patent-rankings.

9. Hashimoto, Takeshi, and Yusho Cho. "China Triples US in Blockchain Patent Filings." *Nikkei Asian Review*, Nikkei Asian Review, 20 Nov. 2019, asia.nikkei.com/Business/China-tech/China-triples-US-in-blockchain-patent-filings.

10. Lin, I-Ting Shelly. "The Robotics Industry in China." *China Briefing*, 9 Dec. 2019, www.china-briefing.com/news/chinas-robot-industry/.

11. Ng, Teddy, and Jane Cai. "China's Funding for Science and Research to Reach 2.5 per Cent of GDP." *South China Morning Post*, 11 Mar. 2019, www.scmp.com/news/china/science/article/2189427/chinas-funding-science-and-research-reach-25-cent-gdp-2019.

12. Radu, Sintia. "Which Countries Spend the Most on Research and Development?" *U.S. News & World Report*, U.S. News & World Report, www.usnews.com/news/best-countries/articles/2018-11-09/these-countries-are-the-top-spenders-on-research-and-development.

13. Gilder, Andrew, et al. "How China's Financial Liberalization Can Unlock New Opportunities." *EY*, EY, 7 Nov. 2019, www.ey.com/en_us/banking-capital-markets/how-china-financial-liberalization-can-unlock-new-opportunities.

14. EY. *Financial liberalization in China: How inbound financial institutions should strategize.* EY, 2019.

15. "Latest China Regulatory Updates - China Further Opens up Financial Sector (VIII)." *EY*, www.ey.com/cn/en/industries/financial-services/ey-pov-china-further-opens-up-financial-sector-viii.

16. "Insurance Association of China Says Market Share of Foreign Insurers Has Risen." *Reuters*, Thomson Reuters, 20 June 2019, www.reuters.com/article/china-insurance-idUSB9N1PJ04R.

CHAPTER THREE

1. "Cryptocurrency Market Capitalizations." *CoinMarketCap*, coinmarketcap.com/.

2. Li, Kenny. "The Blockchain Scalability Problem & the Race for Visa-Like Transaction Speed." *Hacker Noon*, 28 Apr. 2020,

hackernoon.com/the-blockchain-scalability-problem-the-race-for-visa-like-transaction-speed-5cce48f9d44.

3. Leibowitz, Matt. "EOS: Don't Believe The Hype." *Medium*, Medium, 1 Aug. 2018, medium.com/@matteoleibowitz/eos-dont-believe-the-hype-c472b821e4bf.

4. Higgins, Stan. "From $900 to $20,000: Bitcoin's Historic 2017 Price Run Revisited." *CoinDesk*, CoinDesk, 30 Dec. 2017, www.coindesk.com/900-20000-bitcoins-historic-2017-price-run-revisited.

5. Nair, Vinay. "What Will The Fourth Generation of Blockchain Look Like?" *Hacker Noon*, 10 Aug. 2019, hackernoon.com/what-will-the-fourth-generation-of-blockchain-look-like-daa5a4e90c59.

6. Kauflin, Jeff. "Where Did The Money Go? Inside the Big Crypto ICOs of 2017." *Forbes*, Forbes Magazine, 21 Feb. 2019, www.forbes.com/sites/jeffkauflin/2018/10/29/where-did-the-money-go-inside-the-big-crypto-icos-of-2017/#29ff4c0b261b.

7. Alethio. "A Retrospective of the EOS Token Sale." *Medium*, ConsenSys Media, 12 Aug. 2019, media.consensys.net/a-retrospective-of-the-eos-token-sale-172d3437932b.

8. Dale, Brady. "EOS Revisited: Investors Take Another Look at the Longest-Running ICO." *CoinDesk*, CoinDesk, 9 May 2018, www.coindesk.com/eos-revisited-investors-taking-another-look-longest-running-ico.

9. Rooney, Kate. "A Blockchain Start-up Just Raised $4 Billion without a Live Product." *CNBC*, CNBC, 1 June 2018, www.cnbc.com/2018/05/31/a-blockchain-start-up-just-raised-4-billion-without-a-live-product.html.

10. LastWeekTonight. "Cryptocurrencies: Last Week Tonight with John Oliver (HBO)." *YouTube*, uploaded by LastWeekTonight, Mar 11. 2018, www.youtube.com/watch?v=g6iDZspbRMg.

11. Baraniuk, Chris. "Bitcoin's Energy Consumption 'Equals That of Switzerland'." *BBC News*, BBC, 3 July 2019, www.bbc.com/news/technology-48853230.

12. "Blockchain Software Architecture." *EOSIO*, eos.io/.

13. Samani, Kyle. "EOS ($EOS) Analysis and Valuation." *Multicoin Capital*, 24 Apr. 2018, multicoin.capital/2018/04/24/eos-analysis-and-valuation/.

14. Gencer, Adem Efe, et al. "Decentralization in bitcoin and ethereum networks." *International Conference on Financial*

Cryptography and Data Security. Springer, Berlin, Heidelberg, 2018.

15. Xu, Brent, et al. "Eos: An architectural, performance, and economic analysis." (2018).

16. Hertig, Alyssa. "Loveable Digital Kittens Are Clogging Ethereum's Blockchain." *CoinDesk*, CoinDesk, 7 Dec. 2017, www.coindesk.com/loveable-digital-kittens-clogging-ethereums-blockchain.

17. Dale, Brady. "'One Network, Many Chains' – The Case for Blockchain Interoperability." *CoinDesk*, CoinDesk, 30 Jan. 2020, www.coindesk.com/one-network-many-chains-the-case-for-blockchain-interoperability.

18. "Security Tokens vs. Utility Tokens - How Different Are They?" *Hacker Noon*, 28 Apr. 2020, hackernoon.com/security-tokens-vs-utility-tokens-how-different-are-they-22d6be8901c2.

19. "Rampant Collusion in EOS Exposed by Huobi Leak." *Trustnodes*, 29 Sept. 2018, www.trustnodes.com/2018/09/29/rampant-collusion-in-eos-exposed-by-huobi-leak.

20. O'Neal, Stephen. "Corrupt Governance? What We Know About Recent EOS Scandal." *Cointelegraph*, Cointelegraph, 5 Oct. 2018, cointelegraph.com/news/corrupt-governance-what-we-know-about-recent-eos-scandal.

21. Huillet, Marie. "EOS RAM Prices Skyrocket Amid Network Speculation." *Cointelegraph*, Cointelegraph, 4 July 2018, cointelegraph.com/news/eos-ram-prices-skyrocket-amid-network-speculation.

22. Zalatimo, Salah. "Why We're Here: A Letter from Our CEO, Salah." *Voice*, 18 Mar. 2020, voice.com/blog/why-we-are-here/.